THE GREEN FUSE

POETRY 9: Allen Ginsberg, Victor Bockris (third from left), William Burroughs, John Giorno, Lita Hornick

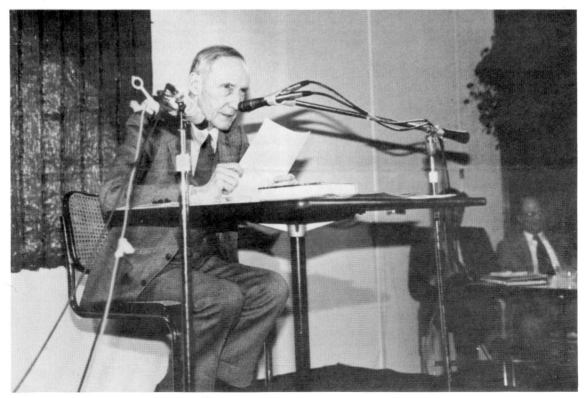

William Burroughs   Museum of Modern Art 1980

THE GREEN FUSE
A MEMOIR

Lita Hornick

GIORNO POETRY SYSTEMS

THE GREEN FUSE by Lita Hornick

Copyright by Lita Hornick 1989

Published by GIORNO POETRY SYSTEMS
222 Bowery
New York, N.Y. 10012

Book Store & Library Distribution
Small Press Distribution
1814 San Pablo Ave.
Berkeley, CA 94720

ISBN—1-877957-00-3

Printed in the USA by
Capital City Press, Inc.
Montpelier, VT 05602

Cover by Mark Michaelson

CONTENTS

FOR MYSELF

THE FORCE THAT THROUGH THE GREEN FUSE DRIVES THE FLOWER

The force that through the green fuse drives the flower
Drives my green age; that blasts the roots of trees
Is my destroyer.
And I am dumb to tell the crooked rose
My youth is bent by the same wintry fever.

The force that drives the water through the rocks
Drives my red blood; that dries the mouthing streams
Turns mine to wax.
And I am dumb to mouth unto my veins
How at the mountain spring the same mouth sucks.

The hand that whirls the water in the pool
Stirs the quicksand; that ropes the blowing wind
Hauls my shroud sail.
And I am dumb to tell the hanging man
How of my clay is made the hangman's lime

The lips of time leech to the fountain head;
Love drips and gathers, but the fallen blood
Shall calm her sores
And I am dumb to tell a weather's wind
How time has ticked a heaven round the stars.

And I am dumb to tell the lover's tomb
How at my sheet goes the same crooked worm.

Dylan Thomas

CHAPTER I

EARLY YEARS

I was born Lita Romola Rothbard on February 9, 1927 in Newark, N.J., an only child. My father was a lawyer; my mother was a house-wife. The Weequahic section of Newark was then a quiet upper middle class Jewish neighborhood. I was a lonely child; and, at a very early age, discovered some of my father's Columbia books in the attic, English classics. I went straight for the poetry and, by the age of nine, was writing poetry myself. At that age, I also wrote a play called "Love Comes to Royalty and Peasants." My poems were imitations of nineteenth century English literature, and, when I was twelve years old, won first prize in a national children's hobby contest. I wrote my last poem at the age of seventeen, a sonnet called "Dry Ice," which was published in the *Barnard Bear* in my freshman year. After that the muse left me, and I tried my hand at story writing.

In my childhood, I had several friends with whom I played familiar children's games, but I also invented imaginary games for us. In my favorite, I was a queen ordering a prisoner to be boiled in oil. The prisoner would then be dragged off delightedly screaming. Some-times, however, my friends would turn on me and vow never to play any of my nutty games again. I would then be alone and go up to the attic to read. My grandmother indulged me by making queen's costumes for me, in which I would traipse around the streets of Newark, earning the reputation of town nut. In my book *Kulchur Queen*, there is a picture of me wearing one of those queen's costumes. This is all I can say about my childhood, which I remember rather dimly. The things I remember most vividly I could never commit to print, out of consideration for my parents.

My adolescence was much brighter and was one of the happiest times of my life. I turned out pretty and was popular with the boys. Also, a tremendous asset, I had big boobs. I started developing breasts at the age of nine; and, at the age of eleven, the year I reached puberty, I was more endowed than many women. I was invited to a teen age party at age eleven; and one of my queen's costumes, which then showed a lot of cleavage, served as an evening dress. It was a beautiful gown of hot pink taffeta with pale green ruching and a hoop skirt. It made a big hit, and I had a wonderful time. There soon began a prolonged argument with my mother about whether the formals I wore to dancing school should show my cleavage or not. I usually won. However, I was just a tease; I was totally pure and untouched.

At the age of thirteen and a half, I entered Weequahic High School. My snobbish parents wanted to send me to a private school in north Newark, then a wasp enclave. I refused at first because I wanted to go to a coed school; but, by the end of my sophomore year, I was beginning to go out with college boys instead of high school boys, and so agreed to enter Prospect Hill Country Day School in the fall. I enjoyed Prospect Hill very much, despite the fact that I had to wear blue uniforms and no makeup or nail polish during the week. I worked very hard, as I was ambitious to get into a good college. I was surrounded by unindustrious Wasp girls, who did not plan to go to college but just to come out. Nevertheless, I felt no antisemitism. Dr. Hamblen, the headmaster, was a dear man who had only three girls in his Latin class. He would write "poor prune" on our papers if we made a mistake. Miss Smith, the headmistress, was a dragon; but she liked me because I was a straight A student and the only girl she could consider sending to Vassar, her alma mater. I told her, however, that I wanted to go to Barnard, because, at the age of twelve, I had determined to marry a New Yorker. She told me I need apply to no other school.

In the autumn of 1944, I entered Barnard College. It was my first real culture shock. The work was much harder, more voluminous and more exciting than that of Prospect Hill; although freshmen still had to take a "hygiene" course that taught that only men needed orgasms because they had to release sperm. Most of the day students at Barnard were Jewish, but the opposite was true of the dorm students.

I was a dorm student. I had friends from all over the world. There was Diana Chang from China, whose poems were published in *Poetry* while she was still in college and who later became a successful novelist. Shirin Devrim was the step-daughter of the regent of Saudi Arabia. When she went out on a date, she was covered with exotic gold jewelry; but she only bathed when she went out and her room stank. There was Betty Jean Kirchner, who later married Robert Jay Lifton, the famous psychiatrist, and Marian Hinn, a pious Protestant from Plainview, Texas, who was always talking about how she and her mother devoted themselves to helping people. Anne Seillére came from a noble French family whose title on her mother's side went back to the Crusades. Her father was an industrialist. Although she was a leftist intellectual at Barnard, she said that when she went home she could not marry out of her class. Last, but certainly not least, was Jeane Jordan, later Jeane Kirkpatrick, and her inseparable companion, Rosa Velasco. It was rumored they were lovers. Jeane was the only one among us who was not an English major; she majored in government. She was the only one among us besides me who later went on to take her Masters at Columbia Graduate School. At Columbia, hearing that I was majoring in contemporary literature, she asked if I ought not to meet a "real live poet." I replied that I would love to, and so she said that she knew one and suggested that we all go down to the San Remo in Greenwich Village where the bohemians hung out. I wish I could remember the name of the young poet she introduced me to; but, in any case, I said something about Baudelaire he didn't like. He then invited me to a contest in drinking boilermakers. I must have lost, because all three of them had to take me home and put me to bed.

The exhiliration of Barnard made me see how narrow and provincial my middle class Jewish background was. I revolted against my parents, particularly my mother, who had a stranglehold on me. I still, however, clung to the belief that I must be a virgin until my wedding night. I had many dates with men, with whom I experimented with necking and petting but did not, as they used to say in those days, "go all the way." I think it was the cruellest and unhealthiest moral code ever invented; but that was what it was like in the forties, and also in the fifties I am told, though I was already married by then. My parents supplied me amply with clothes, furs and jewelry; and, still being a tease, I went to my junior prom wearing a gown consisting of a long black silk skirt, slit to the knee, and a little bra made of red roses. I led a kind of double life at Barnard. When at school, I was a serious student dressed in a sweater, skirt and loafers, with no makeup. When I went out on a date, I put on one of my low cut cocktail dresses, high heels and lots of makeup. I did not go out with any Columbia boys but with grown men, who took me to the Stork Club, El Morocco and the Monte Carlo.

In the beginning of my sophomore year, at the age of 18, I met Maury Delman, the only man I was ever romantically in love with. This sort of thing can only happen once in a lifetime and usually only in youth. He was not at all what one would think of as a good candidate for marriage. Although he was two years older than I, he was in the same grade in school, because he had spent two years in the Marines hitting every beachhead in the South Pacific. He was not interested in studying nor in going into his father's business, the then very fashionable Delman shoes. His father did not, for obvious reasons, think Maury was ready for marriage but said that, if we eloped, he would give us $3,000.00 a year, an income on which we could not possibly live comfortably. Maury asked my father if he would subsidize this income and he refused. My father too did not think Maury eligible for marriage. I refused to elope, not merely for lack of money and security but also because I sensed there was something definitely wrong with Maury, at least for *me* at that very conventional and bourgeois time of my life. He was enthused about a book he called *Against the Grain*, since he read it in English translation. It was not until I got to Columbia graduate school that I discovered what that book was all about. It was *A Rebours* by Huysman. Therefore, in my junior year at Barnard, I went to bed with Maury; although we didn't go any further than finger fucking. I was thus a technical virgin on my wedding night. It was neverthless the best sex I ever had. Maury gave great foreplay and I was in love. After a while the hopeless relationship soured. Maury accused me of sleeping with other men as a pretext for breaking off with me. It was totally untrue, but he had to hurt me to make the break. He asked me to have sex with him one last time, and I refused. It was the most traumatic experience of my life.

I enrolled as an English Composition major and took two years of story writing, because I could not write poetry any more. I was not too good at story writing, because I was never interested in other people's characters and I never noticed my surroundings. I did, however, write a good imitation of Swift, called "A Voyage to Discordia," for my eighteenth century class, which was later published in the *Barnard Bear*. Miss Sturtevant, my story writing teacher, said I ought to be a critic, because I had done so well writing about Joyce and Proust in her class on the novel and because my comments on other people's stories were so much to the point. Therefore, I went to Columbia Graduate School for my masters to learn how to become a critic. Thus began a ten year period of platonic adoration for Professor William York Tindall, who taught Contemporary British Literature from 1885 to 1945. I wrote my masters' thesis on Dorothy Richardson, which Tindall liked very much. He admitted me to his special seminar on *Finnegans Wake*, where we spent the entire semester unraveling two paragraphs.

CHAPTER II

MARRIAGE AND COLUMBIA

The summer I graduated from Barnard I met my husband to be, Morton J. Hornick, a New Yorker of course. We met at the Hotel Mount Washington, a resort in Breton Woods, New Hampshire, where I was staying with my parents. When he came over to talk to me, I was wearing a tight black sweater and a white pleated skirt. We sat under a tree where he says I recited poetry to him for eight hours. It was really only half an hour, but the time grew longer as the story progressed through the years. He says he was filled with admiration and terror. We courted during the year I was taking my masters and were married on June 2, 1949. During our courtship, I was living at the King's Crown Hotel, a Columbia residence right across the street from where Eisenhower lived, president of Columbia at that time. Whenever we attempted to park, a policeman would shine a flash-light into the car. This made it doubly sure that I would remain what they used to call a "Jewish virgin" until my wedding night.

There was a post-war shortage of apartments in New York, and a relative of Morty's owned a small pre-war apartment house in Riverdale into which we moved. There were no high rises in Riverdale then, which was a community of private homes in the Fieldston section and gorgeous estates on the Hudson. On August 3, 1950, our first son, named Louis, was born. In September, I fled back to Columbia for my Ph.D. to escape the horrors of domesticity. I only had a nurse for Louis for six months, though I always had a sleep-in maid. For the first six months after the nurse left, the baby was too young to leave alone with the maid; and I was house bound. I contented myself with studying for the sight reading tests in German and Latin required for matriculation. I had already passed the French test before matriculating for my masters. I reviewed my high school Latin and translated Virgil, on whom I was told the test would be given. I had no German, so I learned it myself from a German grammar, and translated the text book on which I was told the test would be given. I passed both tests at the end of the school year.

The early years of my marriage were the most horrible years of my life. Young people today would ask why I did not get a divorce; but both Morty and I believed you got married forever, for better or for worse. This was a good thing, because we became very close in later years. When Louis was an infant, however, I had to sit in the park with all the stupid, ignorant, bourgeois women, so different from my friends at Barnard. I used to clench my fists and grind my teeth and whisper to myself: "This isn't me, this isn't me, this isn't me! This is not my life, this is not my life, this is not my life!" And so on, over and over again. When Louis was one year old, I left him with the maid two afternoons a week to take two required courses at Columbia, Anglo-Saxon and the History of the English Language. Young women today leave their babies with sometimes inexperienced baby sitters or in sometimes dubious day care centers and go off to work or school with little guilt, but I was born too soon and was ridden with guilt. My humdrum life was softened by dressing up and going out in the evening, for we could always leave the baby with the maid after he was put to bed. The New York City Ballet brightened my life, at the old City Center when Balanchine was at his greatest. Best of all, we began to travel, leaving the baby and the maid at my mother's apartment in East Orange.

At this very early period I began to collect School of Paris Prints, going to auctions occasionally at Park-Bernet when I could spare a little free time. My first acquisition in 1950 was a Bonnard lithograph. My interest in literature had led me into an interest in the other arts and the subject of aesthetics. When I was taking my masters I had audited a course in elementary harmony and counterpoint at Julliard, but found musical theory a specialty unto itself and so did not continue. However, being self taught in art, I didn't have the courage to collect contemporary paintings till much later. When Louis was two, I left him with the maid every afternoon after his lunch. I was always back in time for his bath and supper. When he was three, he entered morning nursery school, and I was free to go down to Columbia all day. I was preparing for my orals. Also, at that time, we took a larger apartment in the first high-rise erected in Riverdale, where we lived comfortably till Blake was born.

I was enthralled by Tindall's class. He opened his lectures by saying: "Three Jews created the twentieth century, Freud, Marx and Einstein." He was a Joyce and Yeats man, and we studied them exhaustively. We also studied all the great writers of the earlier part of the century except Pound. Pound was ignored. Tindall said he was a great critic but not a great poet. It later took *Kulchur* to re-educate me. However, we studied Eliot, Woolf, Lawrence, Auden, Shaw and Wilde and a great many minor writers, my favorite of which was Synge. I was one of Tindall's favorite students and did extremely well in his doctoral seminar. The seminar involved the interpretation of difficult texts with much emphasis on the symbol. We had to read much Freud, and Jung as source material for the literary symbol. The plan at Columbia for doctoral candidates in English was a major field, in my case contemporary British literature, a major figure which might be Shakespeare, Milton or Chaucer, and two minor fields. My major figure was Shakespeare, whom I loved. I adored Prof. Campbell, who was a figure out of the Edwardian era. He hated O'Neil and once whispered to me wickedly: "Do you know what I call *Desire Under The Elms*?" "No, what?" "*Lust in the Dust.*" We studied not only Shakespeare's plays and poems but his sources, the various quartos, the first Folio and the history of Shakespeare criticism. One of my minor fields was medieval literature, which I loved. I had wanted to take aesthetics as my other minor, which would have put me in the philosophy department; but I was warned by Tindall not to cross department lines. I therefore substituted the history of literary criticism from Aristotle to Croce. This involved my reading several books in French which had not been translated. My French was still good enough to do that then, though it isn't now.

At the oral examinations candidates were responsible for an intensive knowledge of all four of their special fields but also might be asked anything in English literature or the works of any great figure in world literature. I worked myself into a frenzy beforehand, as everyone did; since one could not possibly know *everything* and one could not take the examination *twice*! They made it easier by making the first question the subject of one's dissertation, which one was not bound to afterwards. The purpose was to give the candidate an opportunity to choose a subject about which he could speak well. If what he had to say interested the professors, the questions would follow along related lines.

If he seemed unprepared, they would begin firing questions from all sides. I chose to speak about the opposition of Greek/Jew to Roman/Briton in *Ulysses* and proceeded to trace this motif through the great book, chapter by chapter. After a while, Tindall stopped me and asked me some more questions about my major field, which I was fortunately able to answer. He then passed me on to Campbell, who asked if I could trace a motif through a play of Shakespeare's in a similar way. I responded by tracing the imagery of disease and corruption through Hamlet. He then passed me on to the professor of medieval literature who asked if I could do something similar in that field. I chose to trace some themes through the myths on which much of medieval literature is based and then read from Chaucer, in the correct accent, and translated, as was required of every candidate. I took the history of criticism straight. Finally, they asked me to step outside; and, when they called me back, I was told that I had passed with a citation of distinction.

Immediately after that, I became pregnant. We had been trying to have a second child for some time with no result; but, as soon as I passed my orals, I became fertile again. I was determined to have another boy, as I did not want to live my life over again through a daughter; so I started buying blue baby clothes and painted the nursery blue. At the same time, I went down to Columbia well into my ninth month. At that time, I was the only pregnant woman on campus; although there are a great many of them today. I was working on my dissertation on Dylan Thomas, then a highly controversial writer in academic circles. It was to be the first doctoral dissertation ever written on Dylan. On September 22, 1955, Blake was born, named after William Blake of course. Louis had had to be named after Morty's father the founder of the company. We didn't have room for two in help sleeping in; so Morty, who was now being sympathetic toward me, suggested that we keep a permanent nurse and a part time maid. I jumped at the chance of having a nurse. I did not want to be tied down with an infant ever again in my life. The maid came three days a week to do the cleaning and cooked dinner the days she was there. The nurse helped me tidy up on the other days. Morty hated to drive home in the rush hour traffic; so on most of those days I met him downtown for dinner, leaving the nurse to cook for herself and the children. It really wasn't necessary for us to stay in Riverdale as long as we did. Morty was thinking about a house in the suburbs, but I hated the idea. I wanted a large apartment in New York and was determined to hold out in our crowded quarters until I reached my goal.

In the summer of 1956, we went to Europe, the first of our annual, and, later, twice yearly trips. Morty and I were beginning to be very close and loving. We made love in the huge tub at Claridge's, the most elegant hotel in London. When the floor waiter said, in his British accent, "What would madam like?" I said, "This is the place for me." From there we went to Wales. Swansea, Dylan's birthplace, was a hideous mining town. We stayed at the Macworth Hotel, where we had the only room with a bath. Next we went to the beautiful sea-side town of Laugharne, where Dylan later lived, and met his friend, Vernon Watkins. We also went to Suffolk to visit Lady Snow, who wrote under her maiden name, Pamela Hansford Johnson. She had been a sweetheart of Dylan's in their youth. I had corresponded with her and received much valuable information. Amazingly, she gave me two handwritten manuscripts, which now hang framed in our apartment, and lent me a large batch of letters, telling me to post them back to her after I had read them. We then went on to Rome, the French Riviera and Paris. Life was no longer horrible.

In 1958, I defended my dissertation before the examining committee and took my degree. In the same year we moved into a ten room cooperative apartment on Park Avenue with three maid's rooms. I then had room for both a nurse and a sleep in maid and was free to pursue a full time career. However, what career I should pursue was problematical. When I went to see Tindall, he refused to recommend me for a teaching job! I had passed my orals with a citation of distinction, and my dissertation was accepted in the first column. I was certainly qualified. The only explanation I can find is that I was a woman and a woman who didn't have to work for a living. Tindall evidently believed he would be depriving some male, with a family to support, of a job. Wearing my mink coat to one of our conferences had probably been a fatal mistake. He said, "What do you want to teach for? If I didn't have to earn a living, I would never teach. Why don't you just write?" I tried to explain to him that writing scholarly papers could not be done outside the scholarly community, and it was many years since I had done any other kind of writing. He suggested that I take my dissertation to Columbia University Press, but they rejected it on the grounds that Thomas was too controversial a figure to be the subject of a scholarly book. This turned me off writing until 1972 when John Myers published it. I sent it around to my poet friends, who said I should begin writing about *them*. I thus began writing the essays on contemporary American poets, which were later collected in *Kulchur Queen*.

CHAPTER III

KULCHUR MAGAZINE

The years between Columbia and Kulchur were the lost years. I can't imagine what I did with my time except to haunt museums and art galleries, go to the ballet and take out a subscription to the Philharmonic. In 1959, I bought my first contemporary American painting, a Jack Youngerman, from his first show at Betty Parsons. It is an explosion of red on a white ground with heavy paint. It now belongs to the Whitney Museum. I also found a new companionship with Louis, now that he was old enough for me to educate him. He was in all day school; but on Saturdays I began to take him to museums, children's concerts, Gilbert and Sullivan and even the ballet. I read poetry to him every night. I kept a nurse for Blake until he was five and then began to make a companion of him as well. Since the boys were at different stages of development, I had two poetry reading sessions at night. Later on, Blake even helped me to sort and mail *Kulchur*. Despite the myth that the first five years are the most important, my sons grew very close and devoted to me and remain so still. This is probably because I never fed on them like most mothers, especially Jewish mothers. I was never a figure they had to revolt against.

Donald Allen's famous anthology, *The New American Poetry 1945-1960*, turned me on with a great flash of renewed insight. This was an entirely different literature than that I had studied at Columbia. First of all, it was American poetry rather than British; secondly, it began at the date that Tindall's course ended. It was bewildering as well as fascinating, and I realized it was necessary for me to read a great deal more of it. It was also necessary for me to study Pound. I haunted the Gotham Book Mart looking for the material in little magazines, but little of the work had been published. In the fall of 1960, I came across a copy of *Kulchur 2*. It seemed quite interesting and had a flyer enclosed begging for funds. I wrote to the editor, Marc Schleifer, and told him I would send him a donation if he would tell me his future plans for the magazine. I expected to send him fifty or a hundred dollars. I did not expect to meet him and didn't dream I would become publisher of the magazine. However, Schleifer called me up on the day he received my letter, and said he would like to meet me. This filled me with both excitement and alarm. Was I really going to meet a real live beatnik? Nevertheless, I made an appointment for him to come up to my apartment.

Schliefer arrived, seven years my junior, clean shaven and short haired, and wearing Ivy League clothes. I was relieved. I told him about my work at Columbia and the great revelation of the Don Allen anthology. This should have made him realize that I would not want any part of his magazine without a literary interest in it. For his part, he led me to believe that he planned to build *Kulchur* up to the circulation and influence of the prestigious quarterlies. Little did I know that he only wanted backing for #3, which was to be an inflammatory issue, before disappearing into the Cuban revolution. To my amazement, he suggested that I become the publisher. It sounded like a marvelous idea, but I was fearful. I told him I would talk it over with my husband. To my surprise, Morty told me to go right ahead. He knew how unhappy I was without a career. I told him it would lose money; he said that was all right. We had no idea how *much* it would lose. I must pause now to set the record straight about this transaction. Gilbert Sorrentino said in *The Little Magazine In America*, published by Northwestern University and the Pushcart Press, that I told the new editorial board I brought in after Schleifer's resignation (and after I had edited *Kulchur 6 entirely* by myself) that I just wanted to support them and didn't want to have any part of the magazine. Such words never crossed my lips!! I never told Marc Schliefer, Gilbert Sorrentino or any other son of a bitch that I just wanted to support them and didn't want any part of the magazine. What then is the reason for all this confusion? Though Sorrentino can sometimes be vicious and has earned the appelation of "the literary mafioso" or "the big hit man" in certain circles; he has too much character and integrity to be a liar, especially in a document intended for literary history. What seems to be the answer is that Marc Schliefer, who *was* a liar and a creep, fearful that his friends

24

would take a dim view of his bringing a strange woman from Park Avenue into the magazine, told them all that he had a rich broad in tow, who wanted to support him and didn't want any part of the magazine.

And so Kulchur Press, Inc. was formed, of which I was made the president. Marc had not incorporated but had published *Kulchurs 1* and *2* under his own name. The magazine was sold to this corporation, in February, 1961, for $250.00, and Marc was given a contract as editor, a responsibility he did not live up to for very long. I had no objection to his being the editor, as the new literature was still too unfamiliar for me to have a say in the editing at that time. Marc began gathering material for #3, which I did not see until it was in galley proof; while I busied myself with building a subscription list and trying to find a national distributor. During this period, he introduced me to Ted Wilentz of the eighth Street Bookshop and the Becks of the Living Theater. He also arranged for me to give a cocktail party for his friends and most of the New York contributors. When I finally saw the galleys of *Kulchur 3*, I was worried about going to jail, because it was on me, as publisher, that the legal responsibility rested. One would not raise an eyebrow at this material today, but it was a different story in 1961. I told my husband about it, and he was not at all worried. He could not believe that little wifey could get into trouble with the law. He didn't bother to read the galleys himself, but told me if I was *really* worried I should take them down to our lawyers. And so I took the galleys to Eugene Klein of Phillips, Nizer, Benjamin, Krim and Ballon. As Eugene leafed through them, he turned pale. He said, "I'll show them to our pornography expert. Come back tomorrow." The next day he told me, "Our pornography expert says, if you publish these galleys, you will definiteley be arrested by the New York vice squad. You will have to spend at least one night in the Women's House of Detention until we can bail you out. You will lose in every lower court, but we will win in the Supreme Court!" I was agaga; but I took the galleys from Eugene and, after eliminating two items that were really dangerous for that time, I went ahead with publication. Eugene notwithstanding, nothing ever happened to me. The two things I eliminated were Burroughs' now famous routine about Roosevelt, for which LeRoi Jones was arrested at gun point when he published it in *The Floating Bear*, and a story by Paul Goodman drooling over a sailor. These acts of censorship made me Schleifer's bitter enemy, and he bad-mouthed me enough to cause me trouble for years.

While *Kulchur 3* was still in page proof, Schliefer told me he was going to Mexico for the summer and had appointed Gilbert Sorrentino as guest editor of #4. When the issue came out soon after that, I made my legendary voyage from Park Avenue down to the Blue Yak bookstore on Tenth Street, with a shopping bag full of *Kulchur 3*. Rochelle Owens insists that I wore a pink wool suit with a matching pill box hat. I tell her she has me mixed up with the outfit Jackie Kennedy wore at Jack's assasination. I insist I wore a red wool dress, with matching stole, and a black patent leather hat. In any case, the poets there were stupefied at my bourgeois outfit. As with Tindall, I suspect, my looks were an impediment rather than an asset. The proprietors of the Blue Yak were George Economou, Armand Schwerner, David Antin and Jerome Rothenberg. Together with Robert Kelly and Rochelle, they formed the short lived Deep Image group. After getting over their amazement at my alien appearance, they bought a number of copies of *Kulchur 3*. This issue contains a story by Jack Kerouac called "Dave," a poem by Charles Olson, a selection of the important Yage letters by William Burroughs, scores by George Brecht, an appreciation of Samuel Greenberg by Joel Oppenheimer, short pieces by Gary Snyder, Diane DiPrima, Tuli Kupferberg and Allen Ginsberg, Paul Bowles on Kif, "Milneberg Joys" by Leroi Jones, "Elsie" by Herbert Huncke, "You too go that way" by Joel Oppenheimer, Donald Phelps on pornography, a short piece on the theatre by Julian Beck and reviews.

The next thing I had to do was to secure Sorrentino as editor of *Kulchur 4*, since my instinct told me Schliefer had not really made sure of that. Sorrentino had no phone; and so I arrived one morning at his door, where he appeared, darkly handsome, in pajama bottoms. At first he assumed I had come to his apartment to go to bed with him, but I soon convinced him I had come to ask him to edit *Kulchur 4*. As I suspected, he told me that Marc had made only the vaguest suggestion about it but that he was willing to do it. He also told me that Mexico was only a passing through station for Schleifer, who was bound for Cuba for an indefinite stay. And so Gil set about editing #4, which had longer and more solid pieces in it and was more to my taste than #3. It contains a piece by Paul Goodman, a sizzling attack on mental hospitals by Hubert Selby, under the pseudonymn Harry Black, an essay on the Oz stories by Osmond Beckwith, an essay on the Maximus Poems by Ed Dorn, a piece on black music by LeRoi Jones, an essay on poetics by Ron Loewinsohn, a very important essay on organic form by Robert Duncan, a peice on Chaplin by Louis Zukofsy and reviews.

Gil also helped me arrange the first of my celebrated parties for the avant garde in the fall of 1961, which I continued giving for twenty years until they became too much for me. At this first party, as at all the early parties at the height of the beat movement, the guests from below Fourteenth Street looked like something from another planet to the few bourgeois onlookers I invited. Also, at all the parties while LeRoi was still active in the white world, the population was half black and some of the great jazz musicians played. My two Irish maids stood rooted to the ground. My father, who was a labor lawyer, said it looked like a meeting of the Communist party in the thirties. My mother-in-law, a real sweetheart, walked in, screamed "Niggers!!" and walked right out again. Soon after that, it was time to start work on *Kulchur 5*, since I was determined to make the magazine into a quarterly. I had not heard a word from Marc Schleifer. I asked Gil to edit #5, but he said it took too much time away from his own writing and so asked Fielding Dawson to do it. I approved of Fielding; but Marian Zazeela, then Marc's wife, threw a temper tantrum in the Cedar Bar and said it was up to her to appoint the next editor. Gil and Fee withdrew at her outburst, and Marian appointed Joel Oppenheimer. I was livid! I had entered into no agreement with Marian and was under no obligation to her. I decided to let Joel do #5 but made up my mind that, if I still had not heard from Schleifer, I would edit *Kulchur 6* myself.

Kulchur 5, Spring, 1962, was a good issue and the first to have a national distributor, Eastern News; although I didn't much like working with Joel, because he was the ugliest man I had ever seen. His issue contains a story by Louis Zukofsky, followed by a poem by Olson and a wonderful takeoff on Pound by Kenneth Koch, then Gil on Williams' *Spring And All*, LeRoi's great essay on tokenism, some of Celia and Louis Zukofsky's translations of Catullus, a brief satire on Aesthetic Realism, A. B. Spellman on blues, Larry Kornfeld on the theatre, Peter Martin on cartoons, reviews and, lastly, Frank O'Hara's first Art Chronicle for *Kulchur*. My art collecting continued at the same time;

27

and I acquired, among other things, my Kenneth Noland target painting, *Night Sound*, which I have since given to the Museum of Modern Art.

Since I did not hear from Schleifer, I plunged in and edited *Kulchur 6*, Summer, 1962, myself. This issue has a cover and a picture portfolio from the Living Theatre. It contains an essay on current English poetry by Denise Levertov, impressions of the City by Roy Fisher, a polemic on the theatre by Julian Beck, an important exchange of letters on poetics by Jerome Rothenberg and Robert Creeley, a poem by Robert Kelly, an Art Chronicle by Frank O'Hara, Liner Notes by the composer Morton Feldman, an essay on film criticism by Donald Phelps, Zukofsky's great play "Arise, Arise," never before published, and film reviews by Fee Dawson. Unfortunately, I did not yet have the contacts to assign book reviews. While #6 was in page proof, Schleifer returned, resigned from the magazine and sold me his back copy inventory of *Kulchurs* I and II. I have never seen nor heard from him since. After that, I then regarded the magazine as totally *mine* to do with as I pleased! The editorial board I brought in at that time, had no legitimate claim on the magazine, though they certainly *thought* they did. This editorial board consisted of LeRoi Jones as music editor, Gilbert Sorrentino as book editor, and Frank O'Hara as art editor. With my consent, Frank brought in Joe LeSueur as theatre editor and Bill Berkson as film editor. I modestly took the title of managing editor, though what exactly went into each issue, then fell to me. LeRoi took his responsibilities the most seriously and was my best friend among the editors.

Kulchur 7, Autumn 1962, contains Ed Dorn's "Notes More or Less Relevant to Burroughs and Trochhi," followed by Gael Turnbull on Roy Fisher. Bill Berkson provided the Art Chronicle, as Frank was too busy, followed by an interview with Lester Young by Francois Postif, LeRoi on Bobby Bradford, a sentimental little piece by Fee Dawson, Joe's first Theatre Chronicle, Zukofsky's great "Five Statements for Poetry," reprinted from the objectivist issue of *Poetry*, and both book and record reviews. About this time, beautiful Michael McClure sent me an essay called FUCK. It wasn't really about fucking but about the importance of bringing the Anglo Saxon words back into the language. I was anxious to publish it but wrote to Michael that the postal inspectors would never read it but, when they saw the word FUCK in bold type, would simply impound the magazine. I expected him to write back, "Bourgeois dog! Censorship! Censorship! Censorship!" However, Michael, quite reasonably, suggested that we spell the title in Greek; and so it came out in *Kulchur 8* as Phi Upsilon Kappa.

Kulchur 8, Winter 1962, begins with an essay on the English scene by Anselm Hollo, who didn't find it very exciting, followed by a misdirected blast at Pop Art by Sorrentino, Joe's Theatre Chronicle, a letter to the editors by Denise Levertov, in which she apologizes for treating Ian Hamilton Finlay too lightly, another little piece by Fee Dawson, a musical setting for one of his father's poems by Paul Zukofsky, Marshall Royal interviewed by Stanley Dance, Cid Corman on Creeley's *For Love*, "Phi Upsilon Kappa," "Five Statements for Poetry Cont." and book and record reviews. The issue contains neither an Art Chronicle nor a Film Chronicle.

Kulchur 9, Spring 1963, was a special play issue edited by Joe LeSueur. The cover was from a drawing by Larry Rivers. Larry called me up and asked me how many plays there were. I replied eight. "Oh good" he said, "Now I can put Shakespeare behind the eight ball." Sure enough, the drawing, when it arrived, proved to be a portrait of Shakespeare with Eight Plays printed underneath it in a circle. I bought the drawing from Larry, and it became part of my growing collection, which soon boasted an Anuskiewicz, and a Wesselmann "Great American Nude." The issue contains short plays, not suited for the stage, by Michael Smith, Arnold Weinstein, Douglas Woolf and Ruth Krauss, followed by the first publication of LeRoi's powerful play "The Toilet," eminently suited for the stage. "The Toilet" is dense with obscenity, but I published it without the flicker of an eyelash. Through *Kulchur* my whole mentality was changing. After "The Toilet," are short plays by Kenward Elmslie, Barbara Guest and Diane DiPrima, followed by Frank' s Art Chronicle, Bill's Film Chronicle, Gil's Poetry Chronicle and LeRoi's record reviews. Gil dragged Jerry Rothenberg's literary reputation through the mud. I was furious and made up my mind to give Jerry a chance to reply.

Kulchur 10, Summer 1963, was an outstanding issue. It has a marvelous photograph of Balanchine on the cover, a picture portfolio from the New York City Ballet and Edwin Denby's essay, "Balanchine Choreographing." All this material was secured by Frank and was, in my opinion, his greatest contribution to the magazine. He only wrote three Art Chronicles for *Kulchur*; though, in his introduction to the *Collected Poems*, Don Allen said that he wrote one for every issue. *Kulchur 10* opens with an essay on poetics by George Oppen, followed by an essay on little magazines by Paul Blackburn, an essay on music by LaMonte Young, "Balanchine Choreographing," Joe's Theatre Chronicle, Bill's Film Chronicle, Zukofsky's "A Statement for Poetry (1950)," Michael Rumaker on Melville, Larry Eigner on Stein, Martin Williams on Thelonious Monk, Sorrentino on Bop and, lastly, reviews. Sorrentino resigned soon after *Kulchur 10* came out, saying he didn't like the direction the magazine was taking! He agreed to stay on as contributing editor. I don't think it was because of Jerry's attack on him, since it was not published until #11. I think it was because he *hated* the dance, and the Balanchine material must have infuriated him. He also hated homosexuals. I accepted his resignation gladly and promptly took over his job assigning book reviews, concentrating on reviewing small press books.

Kulchur 11, Autumn 1963, opens with a brilliant imitation of Swift by W. S. Merwin, followed by Joe on the Theatre of Cruelty, a story by Robert Duncan, musical scores and notes on aesthetics by Morty Feldman, Zukofsky's historic essay on Pound, Walter Lowenfels on the obscure poet, Bob Brown, Ed Dorn on Douglas Woolf, Anselm Hollo on poetics, reviews and, lastly, Jerry's scathing attack on Sorrentino. Frank began to say the magazine should end; and the other editors, LeRoi excepted, began to neglect reading manuscripts.

Kulchur 12, Winter 1963, was supposed to be a civil rights issue; but not enough people contributed on the subject to make a special issue, so most of it was *Kulchur's* usual fare. Bill Berkson dropped out around this time for an extended stay in Europe, but did not formally resign like stately Gil. We remained on good terms, and Morty and I had a good time with him the following summer on the French Riviera. Sensing the editors' growing lack of enthusiasm, I gave myself the title of editor instead of managing editor with this issue. It opens after the brief Rights section, with a wonderful essay on Zukofsky's "A" by Robert Kelly, followed by William S. Pechter on films, a Chronicle of Musicals by Kenward Elmslie, an essay on black language by LeRoi, a short piece by Ed Dorn and reviews. Kennedy was assasinated as the issue went to press; so we tipped in a poem by LeRoi, entitled "To Jacqueline Bouvier Kennedy, Who Has Had To Eat Too Much Shit."

Kulchur 13, Spring 1964, had a cover and picture portfolio by Andy Warhol from his film, "The Kiss," secured for me by my good and loyal friend Gerard Malanga, whom I had first met in 1962. Frank O'Hara had not come through with the cover he had promised, and I didn't dream that Frank and Andy were mortal enemies! The poets never told me any gossip. Alex Katz enlightened me when I was sitting for my portrait by him that spring. At the same time that I was sitting for Alex, Al Held had a studio in the same building, to which Alex brought me. There I acquired the painting *Maltese Cross*, which I helped to name. When Al, who was between galleries, came up to install it in my apartment, I asked him what the title was. He asked, "What do you think it looks like?" I said, "It looks like a Maltese Cross." He said, "Great! The Maltese Falcon was my favorite movie as a kid." *Kulchur 13*, then opens with an essay on measure by George Bowering, followed by an essay on Creeley by Warren Tallman, an essay on Hubert Selby by Gil, Allen Ginsberg's poem "The Change: Kyoto-Tokyo Express, July 18, 1963," a short piece by Douglas Woolf, the pioneer publication of Richard Brautigan's "The Post Offices of Eastern Oregon," Joe's Theatre Chronicle, Peter Hartman on music, film reviews, by Pauline Kael, and book and record reviews. I was doing almost all the work myself by this time; so I terminated the editorial meetings and made all the other editors contributing editors beginning with *Kulchur 14*, I edited the last seven issues of the magazine entirely myself.

At about this time, I began to suffer from insomnia. I was troubled by my relationship with the poets, especially the editors of *Kulchur*, who did not accept me. My doctor at first prescribed sleeping pills but soon suggested that I see a psychiatrist. Unfortunately, he recommended an orthodox psychoanalyst, by the name of Dr. Schapiro. On the first visit I told Dr. Schapiro all about Columbia and *Kulchur*. He said, "This magazine of yours is not a cause of your tensions; it is a symptom." He went on to say that he knew nothing about me except that I had a Ph.D from Columbia, I published a literary magazine named *Kulchur* and I was wearing a very pretty hat. On the next visit he was interested in hearing about nothing but my sex life. He laughed hilariously and mockingly when he learned that I had never had an extramarital affair. There was really nothing seriously wrong with my sex life with Morty except that I preferred to get on top. I could not surrender to the missionary position. Oral sex was always OK, as it is for most women. Nevertheless, Dr. Schapiro, alternating between vulgar brutality and pompous speeches, laughed at me and mocked me. He told me I was afraid of sex, afraid to have an affair and that I could not have sexual satisfaction in an affair without at least two years of "very unpleasant" and very expensive psychoanalysis. Furious with rage, I rose to the challenge. Only days later, I picked up the painter Knox Martin at the Fischbach gallery, where my portrait by Alex Katz was on display. Although we flirted and made sexy eyes at each other, I didn't think, at the time, that I had discovered the candidate for my experiment so quickly and easily.

Kulchur 14 then, published that summer, has a collage by beautiful Joe Brainard on the cover, the first of many works Joe was to do for my publications. It was intended for #13, but was submitted too late for the deadline. *Kulchur 14* was supposed to be a Zukofsky issue; but only Robert Creeley, Jonathan Williams and Charles Tomlinson contributed on that subject. They were followed by a very good story by Mack Thomas, a Grove Press discovery at the time, excellent translations of Vallejo by Clayton Eshlemen, a very good essay by Michael McClure, another piece on an obscure writer by Walter Lowenfels, a piece by Kenneth H. Brown which proved that "The Brig" was more than a director's play and, lastly, reviews.

As I have said, Morty and I took many glorious trips to Europe beginning in 1956. There, although I only collect contemporary art, I steeped my self in the art of the past. On this trip, in the summer of 1964, we decided to travel through what was once the Angevin Empire. We had already done England and saved Normandy for another trip. We thus started out at Tours and proceeded to the abbey of Fontevrault, a twelfth century structure in which some of the Plantagenets are buried. Next we traveled to the castle of Angers. As I stood in front of it, I could not believe it was actually *there* and I was standing there looking at it. It is a massive feudal castle, completely intact and blackened with age. Built in the twelfth century by Henry II, it was rebuilt in the thirteenth century after a fire. Dark, powerful and forbidding, it exudes feudalism. Within are the magnificent twelfth century Apocalypse Tapestries, which were used for centuries to keep the potatoes warm. Traveling south, we stopped at Poitiers, Eleanor's capital and that of Richard Couer de Lion, who considered himself a Poitevin. There we found a Byzantine influenced church and the Salle Des Pas Perdus (Hall of Lost Footsteps), where Eleanor held her courts of love. We passed through Bordeaux and across to Carcassone, a walled and turreted city, surrounding a medieval town and castle. It is so medieval that it is hard to believe it did not come from a movie set. Of course, Violet le Duc put the tops back on the towers; as he restored most of the great medieval monuments of France. We stayed overnight in the little town and then headed for the Cote D'Azur for a rest.

Kulchur 15, Autumn 1964, has a superb essay on Rauschenberg by Nicolas Calas, accompanied by a cover and picture portfolio from the Castelli gallery. Frank O'Hara, as art editor, never brought any art writing into the magazine except his own Chronicles. The issue opens with an important essay on prosody by George Bowering, followed by the Calas piece, an essay on film by my new film critic, Charles Boultenhouse, an essay on music by Barney Childs, a story by Rush Greenlee, an unknown recommended to me by Don Allen, two funny plays by John Fergus Ryan, another unknown, later to become a successful commercial writer, a piece by Walter Lowenfels, a very important essay on Burroughs by Donatello Manganotti and, finally, a great many book and record reviews.

Not long after *Kulchur 15* was published, I met Knox Martin again at the Fischbach gallery, where our flirtation continued. He invited me on a tour of the openings that evening, but I told him I was expected home for dinner. Making sexy eyes at him, I said, "I hope I will see you again some time." Some time later, his dealer, the director of the Fischbach gallery at the time, called me up and said he would like to take me up to Knox's studio to look at his paintings. I accepted. As we drove up to his loft in a godforsaken neighborhood near the Columbia Presbyterian hospital, I was impressed by the fact that it seemed like a "safe" place to have an affair. No one, I thought, would ever see me come and go. When we arrived, Knox and I began to flirt so openly that we were practically necking, to the visible consternation of the director of the Fischbach gallery. No paintings were shown to me. I did not hear from Knox for a few days after that and, as always when I have made up my mind about something, I wanted to get the show on the road. I therefore called him up and invited him up to lunch on the pretext of doing a *Kulchur* cover. There I seduced him. I couldn't let him go ahead and make love to me in my apartment, because one of my maids was walking down the foyer with the handyman to put in a light bulb, and Blake was on his way home from school. I therefore arranged to meet him the next week at his loft. The first time I went up there, the sex was unsatisfactory. He came too quick for me, and I still didn't like the missionary position. The second time was a repeat performance of the first. Visibly annoyed by the unsatisfactory sex, Knox turned to me and said, "You have a nice face. . ." I saw that what was coming was everything he did not find nice about me. Angrily, I thought, "Did I have to let this guy fuck me and risk my whole marriage just to listen to this kind of shit?!" I therefore said, "I guess I've overstayed my time!", got up, got dressed and left.

I was considerably depressed by the outcome of my experiment, because it looked like I had proved Dr. Schapiro right. I toyed with the idea of trying it with another man but thought that that might provoke too much gossip. Little did I realize that Knox had already blabbed it to everyone in the world that would listen to him. I certainly was naive and stupid in those days. Fortunately, Marilyn Fischbach called me up and asked me if I still wanted Knox to do a cover for *Kulchur*. I interpreted that to mean that he was still interested and that I would be able to give my experiment one more try. I told Marilyn that *Kulchur 16* was about to come out, that *Kulchur 17* was already filled and that it would have to wait for *Kulchur 18*. She said that Knox would do a drawing for the cover and that Nicol Calas would write an essay about his art. This sounded good for the magazine, so I said OK.

That season, I made my annual party the reception after the opening of LeRoi's plays "The Toilet" and the "The Slave," of which I was the chief backer. I tried to hold the number of guests within limits, but it was hopeless. LeRoi had his guest list, *I* had a guest list, Larry Rivers, who did the sets, had his list, the producer and the director had theirs. The Pinkerton guard estimated that four hundred and fifty people passed through the door. It was like the subway at rush hour. When Morty and I awakened the next morning, our apartment looked like it was hit by a bomb. When we first moved to this apartment, my mother-in-law, formerly a widow, remarried and moved from her large West End Avenue apartment to Fifth Avenue. She thereupon dumped all her old funiture on *us*. Morty loved it; he was very sentimental about his former home. I *hated* it. It was eighteenth century Jewish. My rage and hatred, which I suppressed, were nevertheless so great that I would sometimes get up in the middle of the night and carve obscenities on the bottom of the dining room table with a razor blade. After LeRoi's party, most of the fake eighteenth century furniture was destroyed but, fortunately, none of the paintings. Morty then told me I could redecorate according to my own taste. I therefore had all the walls painted white and furnished most of the apartment *sparsely* with the classics of modern design. At the same time, the management of the building brought in power from the street to enable the cooperative owners to install through the wall air-conditioners. Therefore, we were able to install not only the air-conditioners but also flood lights in the ceilings to light the paintings evenly, without the shadows cast by lamps, chandeliers or wall sconces. I realize that fashionable taste has now veered away from this kind of austere decor among the nouveau hot shot collectors, but *my* taste will never change. At that party Andy Warhol came with John Giorno, who was the star of Andy's first movie *Sleep*. Everyone knew that Andy wore a wig, but nobody knew for sure. Willard Maas decided to pull Andy's wig off. He went up to Andy and grabbed hold of his hair at the top of his head, froze for a minute, and then let go. Willard found out it was a wig, and saved Andy the embarassment.

To return then to *Kulchur. #16*, Winter 1964, has some powerful drawings by Al Held, unfortunately unaccompanied by a critical essay; but Al's drawings are strong enough to stand alone. I bought the cover drawing from him. The issue contains two poems by LeRoi, followed by Robert Creeley, interviewed by Charles Tomlinson, Jack Hirschman on Mallarmé and "Exercises" by Nicol Calas. Next I began bringing in the future with Andy Warhol, interviewed by Gerard Malanga, followed by Martin Williams on television, Charles Boultenhouse on the theatre, my good friend's Rochelle Owens' great poem in prose and verse, "Elga's Incantation," Soren Agenoux on the grim aspects of our culture, Wallace Thurston on the films of Charles Boultenhouse, a letter to Robert Kelly by John Keys and, lastly, reviews.

Kulchur 17, Spring 1965, has Robert Indiana's striking painting "DIE" for a cover, from the series EAT, LOVE, DIE. It is part of a picture portfolio illustrating the essay, "Pop Art, New Humanism and Death" by Carl Belz. The other paintings illustrating this interesting essay are "Black and White Disaster," "Burial" and "Silver Disaster", by Andy Warhol, and "Couch" by Bruce Connor, which displays a disintegrating corpse. The issue opens with Calas on the image, followed by the Belz piece, a poem by LeRoi, more translations of Vallejo by Clayton Eshlemen and a story by John Fergus Ryan. Once more I brought in the future with Ron Padgett's hilarious spoof on form called "Sound and Poetry," followed by Matthew Andrew's Theatre Chronicle, Charles Boultenhouse's Film Chronicle and book reviews. There were to be no more jazz reviews contributed by LeRoi who, in Ed Dorn's magazine, *Wild Dog*, called me a pretentious, bourgeois white lady. The poetry anthology promised by LeRoi as a special issue, and never completed, was announced in this issue. It was eventually done as the first *Kulchur* book by his ex-wife, Hettie.

Soon after the publication of *Kulchur 17*, Knox called me up and told me that the cover for *Kulchur 18* was ready. I asked if Nicol's essay was also ready and was told that it had not come through and that two poems by an unknown friend were to be substituted. I was furious but held my peace. Knox suggested that we meet at the Museum of Modern Art, although he knew very well that I did not want to be seen in public with him. His voice had a nasty edge and I scented danger, so decided to humor him. When we met at the MOMA, I learned, to my barely concealed rage, that instead of an abstract drawing, I was presented with a photograph of *himself* standing in front of one of his paintings. The picture portfolio contained paintings of weird pop-eyed birds or, as David Antin wrote in a later issue of *Kulchur*, "hyper thyroid birds." The two poems by David Ross bore no relation to the paintings that I could see. I felt I had no choice but to accept this obnoxious material. *Kulchur 18* was about to go to press and I needed a cover. I was so obsessed with *Kulchur* at that time that neither sensitivity nor common sense could possibly have persuaded me to let an issue of the magazine come out late.

The next and last time I went up to Knox's loft, he must have been sitting in his orgone box all morning, because he fucked me for a long time and banged me around in so many different positions that I finally came with him. This was followed by oral sex which, as usual, was OK for me. Congratulating myself at having obtained my objective, I prepared to quit; but, as I arose to dress, Knox started dragging me toward the window. He wanted me to go out on the balcony with him naked and look at the scenery. The only scenery there was were dilapidated buildings and rubble, and the balcony was no more than a fire escape. Now I can't be sure of this; Knox might have been just nutty enough to really want to go out on the "balcony" in the nude and look at the "scenery." I, however, merely assumed that he wanted to have me photographed with him naked so that he could blackmail me. Pulling away in anger and fright, I dressed quickly, ran down the many flights of stairs, walked at a brisk pace out to Broadway, hailed a cab and, after sinking down in the cab, said to myself out loud, "Thank God that's over!!!"

From many things he said to me, because Morty could never keep his mouth shut, it was clear that he had known about it from the beginning but didn't want me to tell him lest he would have to forgive me and thus encourage further activity of this sort. As if even in my wildest dreams, I would *ever* want to get involved with something like *that* again; as long as I lived!!! After many years, I told Morty all about it, and he raised no fuss.

Kulchur 18, Summer 1965, opens with an interview with Paul Goodman by Morgan Gibson, followed by Charles Boultenhouse on Stan Brakhage. Charles and I, armed with a basket of sandwiches and a bottle of brandy, had gone to see a filming of Brakhage's eight hour epic, "Dog, Star, Man." The film is like an abstract expressionist painting in motion. Every once in a while an image, such as a birth or an act of love, will emerge. Since films are made of objects, you can imagine what a task of cutting and editing it takes to make an abstract film. Charles and I sat through it for six hours, hypnotized by the moving forms and colors. The only reason we left before the end is that we noticed the theatre was empty and we were in a bad neighborhood. The Brakhage essay is followed by an interview with Morton Feldman by Robert Ashley, Margaret Randall on the poetic line, two poems by David Ross, poem plays by Ruth Krauss, including a takeoff on the last chapter of Ulysses, a satire on Denise Levertov by Felix Pollak, a story by Joe Brainard, the first half of Armand Schwerner's essay on Wallace Stevens, an Art Chronicle by David Antin (once again the future), a Theatre Chronicle by Matthew Andrews, a satire on Albee by Bob Charbon and reviews.

As I looked over *Kulchur 18*, I realized, to my horror, that Ruth Krauss' takeoff on Molly Bloom might be taken as a confession of my affair. I had accepted this piece before I had ever gone to bed with Knox. The idea that my sacred book, *Ulysses*, would be identified with this abortive, little affair or that I could ever have identified *myself* with the incarnation for our time time of the Great Goddess, Molly Bloom, was enough to make me shudder. There was nothing I could do about it. When I went to pick up my returns for *Kulchur 20* at Eastern News, *Kulchur 18* was still in the window instead of the current issue. Soon after its publication Morty and I took one of our greatest trips, which put this fiasco temporarily out of my mind. We went to Turkey and visited Troy and Pergamum. Although there was nothing to see at Troy but rubble, I was carried away by the very thought of my actually being there in this place of legend. When we crossed the Hellespont, I almost lost my mind.

In *Kulchur 19*, Autumn 1965, with the help of the late great poet, Ted Berrigan, I brought in the future as never before. The issue opens with Ron Padgett's hilarious story, "Bill," followed by Ted's poem about an academic poet on a reading tour, called "A Boke," which I take to be a pun on book and joke, Tom Veitch's marvelously obscene "Yoga Exercises," Ted's Art Chronicle, the refrain of which is "get the money," Ron's word and picture sequence, "Pere Ubu's Alphabet," the second half of Armand's essay on Wallace Stevens and "Two Scenes from the 'The Bingo'" by Dick Gallup. After this brilliant representation from C Press comes Andrews' Theatre Chronicle, a Film Chronicle by Yale M. Udoff and copious reviews.

This triumphant issue was accompanied by two triumphs in art collecting, the acquisition of Frank Stella's "Fez 2," a green and orange striped painting mathematically conceived, and Ellsworth Kelly's masterpiece, "Red Blue." Despite all this, I began to receive some strange manuscripts, grossly misspelled and subliterate. I particularly remember a piece on concrete poetry, which was a crude attack on Allen Ginsberg and the beats. Deeply disturbed, I doubted the authenticity of *all* the manuscripts. I began to think the poets were plotting against me. This made me so ill that I imagined an international conspiracy against me. I saw jeering and threatening messages for me in books and manuscripts, on billboards, buses, trucks and street signs and everywhere imaginable in my environment. I didn't see anything that wasn't *there* but related whatever *was* there to myself through an ingenious system of metaphor. My husband and parents then sent me to a psychiatrist, Dr. Robert S. Mumford, who spent several years talking me out of my delusions. He never succeeded in entirely convincing me about the peculiar manuscripts; but as one suspect after another proved to be a good friend, I decided to let the matter drop instead of trying to get to the bottom of it.

Therefore, in the midst of "the plot," I edited *Kulchur 20*, Winter 1965. No one but my family realized I was ill, as I had tremendous surface control. In #20, fearing that the facts might be distorted, I eliminated most of the essays I was always so fond of, and filled the issue with poems and pictures. It has a cover and picture portfolio of James Waring dancing, illustrating Gerard's interview with Waring. It begins with Ted and Ron's marvelously funny exchange of letters, "Big Travel Dialogues," followed by Gerard's interview, the poem picture sequence by Ted and Ron, "Go Lovely Rose," seven of Ted's great sonnets, some poems by David Ross, a long poem by Armand, an essay on Creeley by Ellen Maslow, a poem by Margaret Randall, an Art Chronicle by David Antin and a great many reviews. With respect to the "Go Lovely Rose" drawings, I intended to convey some kind of angry message to the poets I thought were plotting against me; but, since I neither made the drawings nor wrote the captions *myself*, the message was not very clear or accurate. As I look at these drawings again, I am not sure exactly what I tried to convey through these obscene looking flowers.

CHAPTER IV

THE EARLY BOOKS

After the publication of *Kulchur 20*, I decided to terminate my beloved magazine and substitute poetry books for what had been chiefly a critical journal. Publishing only two books a year and working with only one author at a time, I believed, would alleviate some of the exhaustion I was suffering from. I also reasoned that by *starting* a project that was entirely my own I would get the former editors and their false claims out of my hair. I reasoned, as well, that, if I gave a poet a whole book of his own, he would not submit any subliterate manuscripts for it. I must now apologize to Mary Kinzie, who commissioned my memoir on *Kulchur* for *The Little Magazine in America*. In this memoir, which was also published in *Kulchur Queen*, I wrote that I had terminated the magazine because I was exhausted. This was entirely *true*, but, obviously, not the whole story. I could not write the whole story in 1977, because shadows of "the plot" still lingered in the corners of my mind and I believed it would be too dangerous for me at that time.

In 1966, I was too ill to publish more than one book, the anthology *Poems Now*, edited by Hettie Jones. Morty was very good to me during this period and took the burden of the business end of Kulchur Press off my hands, and turned it over to Seymour Mizels, the treasurer of his company. Seymour has been my right hand man ever since, and I will always be grateful to him. Morty kept me away from too much exposure to people that year and eliminated the 1966 party. While I was yet in the depths, John Bernard Myers, the distinguished art dealer and the publisher of the famous Tibor DeNagy editions, picked me up and befriended me. He and his friend Herbert Machiz, who was a theatre director, were both outrageously witty and obscene queens. They had the funniest act together I have ever witnessed. For many years they gave me friendship, entertainment, intellectual stimulation and happiness. Andy Warhol also lifted me out of the depths of 1966 by offering to do my portrait. Accompanied by Gerard, he took me down to a booth on 42nd Street, which sold three photos for a quarter, and took about five dollars worth of photographs. From these, he selected one photo, blew it up, silk screened it on canvas and painted on it. There are eight 2-foot square canvasses, each with the same image but in different colors. It is the third portrait Andy painted, Ethel Scull being the first and Holly Solomon the second. Today, it is one of the most important paintings in my collection, perhaps even more so than the Ad Reinhardt, bought in the same year and now belonging to the Museum of Modern Art.

Poems Now is a good but not a brilliant book. It harks back, for the most part, to the early period of the magazine and lacks the sizzling writers I introduced in the last issues. Thus it is somewhat retardaire. All the poets, however, are of sterling quality. They include Robert Kelly, Diane DiPrima, Larry Eigner, John Wieners, Joel Oppenhiemer, Kenneth Irby, Ronald Caplan, Sam Abrams, Gilbert Sorrentino, Lorenzo Thomas, Gerard Malanga, Allan Kaplan, Carol Bergé, Tony Towle, John Sinclair, A. B. Spellman, Roger Taus, Ray Bremser, Gerritt Lansing and David Henderson. The cover is by Dominic Capobianco.

Regaining the reins in 1967, I published two magnificent books, which sold out immediately and became collectors items. The first is *Screen Tests* by Gerard Malanga and Andy Warhol. It is composed of poems by Gerard and film stills by Andy. Designed by Andy, it is visually gorgeous. The front and back covers are stunning colored photographs of Gerard, the front in positive, the back in negative. The fifty-four short poems are each written to a person in the fifty-four film stills. Special paper enables one to see the poems through the photographs. The people in the photographs are all celebrities and/or members of the Warhol circle: Paul America, John Ashbery, Benedetta Barzini, Timothy Baum, Marisa Berenson, Ted Berrigan, Anna Buchanan, Debbie Caen, Daniel Patrick Cassidy, Jr., Ronald Cutrone, Salvador Dali, Dennis Deegan, Edwin Denby, Donovan, Harry Fainlight, Giangiacomo Feltrinelli, Charles Henri Ford, Ruth Ford, Allen Ginsberg, Piero Heliczer, Freddy Herko, Jane Holzer, Ed Hood, "International Velvet," Barbara Jannsen, Paul Katz, Sally Kirkland, Kenneth Jay Lane, Billy Linich, Willard Maas, Gerard Malanga, Jonas Mekas, Marie Menken, Allen Midgette, Paul Morrissey, David Murray, Ivy Nicholson, Nico, "Ondine," Ron Padgett, Ronna Page, John Palmer, Gino Piserchio, Lou Reed, Rene Ricard, Barbara Rubin, Phoebe Russell, Francesco Scavullo, Edie Sedgewick, Harold Stevenson, Ronald Tavel, Chuck Wein, John Wieners and Mary Woronov. Gerard's poems are beautiful early Malanga. They are witness to an epoch and a mirror to the world which surrounded Andy during that period, with its connections to the media, high fashion and the beautiful people. One of his most ubiquitous themes is the friends who surround him in an endless round of social life. His attitude toward them is ambivalent, ranging from complete acceptance to dark foreboding. The themes of the photograph album and journal are also prominent, as are illusion and reality, sunlight, flowers and rain.

Bean Spasms by Ted Berrigan and Rob Padgett, with cover and drawings by Joe Brainard, is a triumph of wit, irony and comedy. The great Brainard drawings still hang in my apartment. The book opens with some very funny short pieces in both verse and prose, followed by "Mailman Bill" and "Policeman Dan," takeoffs on children's stories, then "An Interview With Joe Brainard," part nonsense, part satire, part serious interview, next "Boils," collaborations done by rapid free association while many other things were going on, then "Donut, a cartoon," three characteristic poems, "Nancy," a cartoon, "In Three Parts," a work after the early found poems of John Giorno, a Nancy and goldfish cartoon, five more poems, anticipating New York School history, another Nancy and goldfish cartoon, two Dada sonnets, "In Four Parts," a found poem or something resembling one, "Noh," a poem about Yeats, glaciers, mailboxes, Lolita and smells, and "A Personal Memoir of Tulsa, Oklahoma," another rapid association poem. This is all followed by the *completely fabricated* "Interview With John Cage," next one of Ted's great sonnets, five more characteristic poems, two stories under the heading BE BIG, two DOG STORIES, "The Complete Works," a rapid free associative collaboration, LIFE OF A MAN, short poems which anticipate a whole generation, "Some Bombs," a long poem in their characteristic style and the play "Ebbtide," which also anticipates much future literature. Next comes the outrageously funny excerpt from a novel, "Furtive Days," complete with equally funny illustrations, then "Big Travel Dialogues," reprinted from *Kulchur 20*, and, lastly, the long poems, "Tristan Unsalted" and "Bean Spasms."

In September 1967, we went to dinner at Sally and Wynn Chamberlain's on East 77th Street, where I first got to know John Giorno, even though he had been to my big annual parties, and I had first met him at my party in 1963, when he came with Andy Warhol. Also at dinner were Rochelle Owens and George Economou. It was very hot and there was no air-conditioning. At that time John Giorno and Bob Rauschenberg were lovers. Sally was pregnant, and Wynn cooked lamb stew and rice pilaf saturated with hash and marijuana. My head started to go around; and I didn't know what was happening, as I had only had one drink. Rochelle said "Wynn spiked the pilaf with hash. Don't worry! It'll go away in an hour." We all got very high.

In 1967, in addition to the publication of *Screen Tests* and *Bean Spasms*, we acquired our country house, a bauhaus influenced structure designed by Joseph Hoffmann, the father of modern architecture, and executed by Paul Lester Weiner. Reminiscent of Art Deco as well, it was built between 1932 and 1934 for Alma Morgenthau Weiner. It had been unoccupied for seven years when we bought it and restored it to its original form. Naturally, I had the interior painted entirely white, as the architect intended; though the last owner had committed the atrocity of dark green walls, red draperies and a gilt piano. Anticipating my covering the walls with paintings, I at first permitted only four chairs and a coffee table in the middle of the living room. A psychiatrist neighbor called it "hospital pure." Andy Warhol, who loved it, drawled "Geee, this is great. There's nothing here but the television set." John and Herb were the first to come up and introduced us to Lotte Lenye, who lived nearby. She remained a close friend until she died. In 1967, we also gave our annual party again. The jazz musicians having disappeared with LeRoi, Andy brought the Velvet Underground to play that year. They were to be followed in the years ahead by the modernist composers, Phil Glass, Steve Reich, LaMonte Young, Meredith Monk and others. Lastly, at Christmas time, we met Eugene and Barbara Schwartz, the famous art collectors. Since they were wealthy bourgeois people very much involved in the avant garde, film and dance as well as art, they had a healing effect on my mind, making me feel less lonely and more normal.

Soon after we began spending weekends in our house, we began commissioning giant steel sculptures for out of doors. Morty loved these structures for their power, mass, aggression and male energy, and personally supervised their construction and installation. It was wonderful to see one of these sculptures, weighing many tons, lifted high into the air by a crane and then deposited in a concrete foundation. Interest in sculpture led Morty into an interest in painting, and we soon became partners in art collecting. Although, at first, I continued to make the rounds of the galleries myself, and only called Morty in when I was interested in buying something, he became more and more deeply involved. Eventually, we began to go to the galleries together every Saturday.

All was not to run smoothly, however, in 1968. In the spring of that year I "published" a ream of blank typing paper by Aram Saroyan, the son of William Saroyan. I didn't really want to do it, but I had a commitment to Aram. Still haunted by "the plot," I thought he was trying to sabotage my newly successful book publishing venture by forcing me to back out of my commitment and then telling everyone I had gone back on my word because I was too bourgeois to understand Dada. Rising to the challenge, I went ahead and "published" the wretched little thing. My distributor wouldn't touch it; so I sold twelve copies myself and, after saving two copies for history, I threw the rest out in the garbage. I didn't even bother to save the paper for typing. In the same year, however, I published *Silver Flower Coo* by Charles Henri Ford. Charles is mentioned in *The Autobiography of Alice B Toklas* as one of the new talents in Paris at that time. He was about sixteen. He became the lover of Tchelitchef and remained so until Tchelitchef's death, who died in his arms. He remains beautiful still, like the portrait of Dorian Gray. When the surrealists came to America, he became the editor of the important magazine *View*. *Silver Flower Coo*, a mixture of surrealism and pop, is all composed of poem collages. The wrap around cover, unmarred by type, was shot in Andy Warhol's factory, where various members of the avant garde were assembled, myself included. On that afternoon, Andy gave me a complete portfolio of ten Marilyn silk screens as a gift.

I was asked to organize a poetry reading at Wave Hill in Riverdale, a new cultural center on a great estate with a huge mansion, which was formerly the British consulate. The poets I chose were John Giorno, Anne Waldman, and John Perreault. On Saturday, May 31,

1969, we drove to Wave Hill with the poets to choose a site for the readings. From Wave Hill we drove to our country house for lunch. John Giorno and Jasper Johns were lovers at that time, and John drove the poets in Jasper's yellow jeep. Before lunch, we went for a swim in the pool, and the poets took a steam bath in our steamroom. We asked Les Levine to do the poster for the Wave Hill poetry readings. On Wednesday, June 11th, John Giorno drove Les, Anne, and John up to our country house to take the photos for the poster. Les photographed the poets naked in our steamroom. The poster was black and white, 24 X 30 inches, with 36 photographs, each 3 X 5 inches. Through the steam in the steamroon you can see Anne Waldman's big breasts and bush, John Perreault's and John Giorno's cocks, faintly in some photos and clearly in others. The photos are simple, natural, relaxed, and non-erotic. When the Board of Wave Hill saw the poster, they freaked out. They insisted the posters be destroyed. They sent a truck at 10:30 in the morning to get all the posters from John Giorno at 222 Bowery, where they had been delivered. Wave Hill burned them in their incinerator, paid the printer's bill, and cancelled the poetry reading.

On August 14th, 1969 I had lunch with John Giorno, who had just come up from Nags Head, North Carolina, where he and Jasper Johns were spending the summer. Also in that year I published *Luck* by John Perreault, now chiefly known as an art critic. The book looks like a minimalist artwork. It has a dark green cover, unmarred by type, and pale green pages with dark green edges. Though John was not an official member of the second generation New York School, his style reflects it. In the first section, "Houseboat Strip," the poet leaps airily from image to discontinuous image. The method is surrealist, but the tone is much lighter than classical surrealism. In this, it is typical of much poetry of the period. The poems of the second section, "Readymades," are tongue in cheek, straight faced found poems. John was soon to carry this style into performance art. The short poems in "Untitled" revert to New York School surrealism. "New Poems" contains sound poems and lists. Finally, "Current Events" contains forms characteristic of the experimental writing of that time and the time to come, such as sound poems, found poems, lists and performance pieces.

In 1969, I also published *Album* by Kenward Elmslie, with a wonderful cover and drawings by Joe Brainard. The twenty-two Brainard minatures are now in my New York apartment; the other drawings are in my country house. Kenward is a first generation member of the New York School; and his works are campy, witty and elegant. He has also written librettos for operas and musicals; hence many of his works are lyrical. Fortunately, with this book, type was restored to the cover and spine of Kulchur books. The first section opens with some short works in which the leaps from image to image are as rapid as a roller coaster, followed by "The Black Capsule," a cartoon by Kenward and Joe, and then the very funny "Barbie and Ken." There follows a series of lyrics with drawings by Joe, "Ken's Romance," some short poems, in Kenward's adrenaline style and then a play, "The Aleutians." Poems, stories, plays and cartoons follow, in the same style, and then some very musical song lyrics, a "Narrative" for Stravinsky's "L'Histoire Du Soldat Suite," and the extremely witty play in collaboration with James Schuyler, "Unpacking The Black Trunk." After more poems and cartoons, the book closes with "April," diary entries accompanied by Joe's miniatures.

In 1970, Kulchur Press, originally incorporated as a small business, was succeeded by the Kulchur Foundation, a tax exempt cultural and educational institution. Once having attained foundation status, I expanded my gift giving to individuals and institutions in the arts. In that year, I published *Interlocking Lives*, by Kenneth Koch and Alex Katz. This book is a tour de force containing twenty-one drawings by Alex. These same drawings accompany five different stories by Kenneth, yet seem to fit each of the five stories. Kenneth almost drove me crazy with constant rewriting while the book was in progress. On the eve of the Gotham Book Mart publication party, he called me up to ask what terrible thing was wrong with his book, I assured him nothing was wrong. Finally, the party took place and everything went off smoothly.

In 1970, I also published *Balling Buddha* by John Giorno, soon to become one of my best friends. This was my first shocking book in a long time, and I loved it. The wrap-a-round cover by Les Levine, in green, yellow and orange, is derived from a photograph of John's tongue; and the pages are 6 signatures of 32 pages each in 6 colors: yellow, magenta, green, orange, blue, and red. The poems are: "Balling Buddha", "Johnny Guitar", "Cunt," "Purple Heart", "Lucky Man," "Groovy & Linda", "Give it To Me, Baby," "Rose", "Cycle", "Chrome", and descriptions of his Electronic Sensory Poetry Environments from 1966–69. In double columns, based on found phrases, with hypnotic repetitions, he chants and intones. The poems present us with a panorama of images drawn from contemporary life, though images drawn from Buddhism abound. His repetitions are partly a sound structure and partly a device for slowing down the flow of images in order to evoke a state of higher awareness. By his own admission, Giorno is a political poet, yet the influence of Warhol's cool and deadpan images of disaster is obvious. Evocations of brutal violence rivet our attention. Police brutality and the Viet Nam War are prominent themes, though universal human suffering and interior hells are also important subjects. Sometimes homosexual, sometimes heterosexual, sometimes brutal, sometimes joyous, John's sexual passages reach a new level of anatomical accuracy. Sex runs the gamut of all worlds, from hell to heaven; as John tells it like it is. Conspicuous too are themes from the worlds of commerce and fashion. It is difficult to say whether these images present a satirical attitude or one of non-commital acceptance. Again the influence of Warhol is evident. In sharp contrast are the references to religion, myth, the cosmos and the occult. In a completely original form, these poems present both the forces of darkness and the forces of light.

In 1971, I published *No Hassles* by Anne Waldman, with wrap-a-round cover by Brigid Polk and artwork by Joe Brainard, Donna Dennis and George Schneeman. There are also collaborations with other artists and writers. As many have observed, Anne at this early period, writes insouciantly about the everyday life around her. Nevertheless, her work is drawn from much wider spiritual sources than daily life in New York City. This book marks a transition from the more cheerful early poems to a sense of the tragic in more recent work. In an interview with me, however, she stated that there is a great deal of continuity between the two periods. Despite the joie de vivre attributable to a very fortunate upbringing, there is sadness in the earlier poems and humor in the later work. "Writing the Giant Works" typifies the freshness of her early perceptions. "Getting the Light" reveals her humor. In this piece, she and Lewis Warsh throw their clothes overboard on an ocean liner in order to lighten their load. "The Birthday Party" and "The Reading" are memorable accounts of life among the New York poets. "Woman" is an enchanting story of a chance encounter with Linda Schjeldahl on the street. "100 Memories" and "Embarassing Moments" are list poems, and reveal a close connection to the writing of Joe Brainard. "6:09," on the other hand, shows the darker side of Waldman's vision. In this book she deals with both the familiar and the profound, and proves herself a myriad woman. On March 23rd, I had lunch with John Giorno at La Caravelle. John was about to leave for a 6 month trip to India.

In 1971, I also published *Selected Writings* by Joe Brainard, with cover and end papers by Ron Padgett. The cover was a muted peach, which Ron said reminded him of the 30's. The type and end papers are a rich deep blue. I remember, after the book was printed, that Ron called me on the phone very angry at some slight change the printer had made in the arrangement of type on the spine. I cannot remember what the change was. I don't think Ron is angry any more; I don't even know if he remembers the incident. In "Diary Aug. 4th-15th," Joe goes to the Museum of Modern Art both to see the mummified remains of Cleopatra's asp and also King Arthur's sword, Excalibur. He finds them both "interesting objects," but decides to go up to the Metropolitan to see the "real treasures of yesterday," major and minor. After thinking it over, he decides that Excalibur might just as well have belonged to Prince Valiant or Flash Gordon, and is definitely minor. He is thus moved to return to MOMA to see the asp, again, but finds it has been returned to India. Fade to pondering on the fact that Sam Francis has made a painting called "Big Red," which has the same title as a comedy series by Disney. He then paints ten pictures called "Big Red," but decides that only one is major. He is about to destroy the other nine, but reconsiders, and decides that five of them might be considered minor. These he gives to friends, one of whom is Ted. "Back in Tulsa Again" is a hilarious account of a trip from New York to Tulsa taken by Joe and Ron and Ron's wife, Pat. The car is driven by Ron's father, who looks like John Wayne and wears expensive cowboy boots. Despite the innocent tone of its presentation, this is a modernist story, because "John Wayne's" mad descent into Tulsa seems to have happened at least twice, and it also includes a "A List For The Sake Of A List." There follow two marvelously ironic vignettes: "Smoke More" and "Johnny." In "Smoke More," Joe tells us that what is wrong with people is that they don't smoke *enough*. He smokes four packs a day and is proud of it. It doesn't matter, he assures us, if you get cancer, because "If you are going to do something you may as well do it right." The two things he can't stand are people who smoke menthol cigarettes and those who don't smoke at all. "Johnny" is the story of Johnny Pain, who was born with no legs or abdominal region, yet grew up to be successful in all fields of endeavor and always had a sunny disposition. After two Nancy stories, "Marge" and "People Of The World Relax," there comes "Aug. 29, 1967," a rambling account of Joe's impressions of a morning on Kenward's lawn in Calais, Vt. "Sick Art" is not about what the bourgeois considers "sick art" but about what he considers "great art." In "Jamaica, 1968," Joe is not too enthused about the tropic isle. In "What Is Money?", he says, "There is an old saying that money is the root of all evil, there are two sides to every coin." In "Death," he says, "Death is many different things to many different people. I think it is safe to say, however, that most people don't like it." Finally, in "Autobiography," the last piece in *Selected Writings*, he sums up all the important themes in the book.

In 1972, my doctoral dissertation on Dylan Thomas, *The Intricate Image*, was published by John Myers, under the imprint Gallery Editions. Because he had broken with Tibor and opened his own gallery, he did not publish it under the Tibor DeNagy imprint. Approval from the poets set me writing the essays which were to be collected in *Kulchur Queen*. In that year, I published *I Am the Babe of Joseph Stalin's Daughter* by my very good friend, Rochelle Owens, with cover and drawings by Rochelle. The provocative title arose from an image of rebirth; Svetlana had recently had a baby daughter. This illustrates the far reaching metaphors which animate the poems. In her interview with me, she claimed that most of her works are poems of renewal. She stressed the importance of intense involvement, claimed to be in the tradition of the prophets and mystics and maintained that her emphasis on the primal gives her the opportunity of depicting situations where nothing has to be destroyed to be made new. Of sex and eating, recurrent themes in the work, she said they comprise the basic human energy dynamic. Of the superwoman, one of her most important subjects, she said everyone must be conscious of authentic feminist consciousness, if it is not swamped by sociological rhetoric. She wants her poems to project "primal immediacy" and said, "Poems are entities of magic." The title poem for this book illustrates her concern for the primordial. "The Queen of Greece," who is beautiful and las-

1945

1958

1958
With Morty at La Reserve

1960

1960

1977
Front Cover of *Kulchur Queen*
Photo By Les Levine

1977
Back Cover of *Kulchur Queen*
Photo By Les Levine

1984
Study for Mosaic Portrait
By Ned Smythe

1989
Photo By Jack Shear

1989
Photo By Jack Shear

civious, introduces the figure of the superwoman and Rochelle's preoccupation with exotic cultures. The same theme apppears in the "Deebler Woman" poems, in which a black domestic achieves the status of malign high priestess. References to Yahwe, as well as fierce pagan themes, replete with ritual cruelty, are scattered throughout the poems. Altogether, Owens has produced a body of work of uncommon power. Though often cast in primitive or exotic settings, her works are immediately relevant to us here and now.

In 1972, I also published *Talking* by David Antin, a pioneer book. Besides being a poet and a professional art critic, David has a formidable education in linguistics, musicology, anthropology, philosophy, science and mathematics, as well as literature. His major themes are the ambiguity of truth, the ambiguity of the self and the unreliability of memory. In our interview he spoke of reality as fluid and based on the transactions we undertake with one another. These themes are fully developed in *Talking At The Boundaries*, New Directions, 1976; but I shall only deal here with the Kulchur book. The first piece, "November Exercises," was based on a book to help foreigners learn English. Every day he would pick a phrase from this book and write something. The comic episode of two venerable Chinese sages illustrates the utter ridiculousness of human wisdom. It may also be a dig at Pound, the Chinese Written Character and the whole generation of poets who have worshiped Chinese poetry and Chinese wisdom. Another episode shows the total unrelatedness of two people's actions and the question of what is or is not rational or purposive action. In another, American politics, economics, culture and values are attacked. This is related to Antin's dislike for the *whole sphere* of civilized culture. He then illustrates the subjectivity of all experience and attacks the fundamental premises of scientific knowledge. He comments on the limitations of language and the hopelessness of definitions, the unreality of money, the clichés which form a large part of our language and sums up with the spectacle of modern man attempting to deal with "reality." "3 musics for two voices," is a scenario of a performance piece for him and his wife Ely. It deals with the question of whether it could ever be ascertained if a man could find water with a stick. The experiment never comes to a conclusion; the laws of chance are too great. The third piece, another scenario with Ely, illustrates the inadequacy of the Vietnam war effort, though they are both sympathetic to the effort. The last, and most important piece in *Talking* is "Talking at Pomona," Antin's first talk poem. It was given to a group of art students whose values he wished to challenge. It is an attack on formalist art and art as an illustration of art history. He concludes there are no absolute values in art because there are no absolute values in any human system. On August 6, 1972, John Giorno and Peter Schjeldahl came to the country. We all swam and had drinks by the pool and had lunch inside. John had just returned from the Democratic National Convention in Miami with Abbie Hoffman and Allen Ginsberg, and was about to leave for the Republican National Convention also in Miami.

In 1973, I presented my first series of poetry readings at the Museum of Modern Art. Barbara Schwartz had put my proposal before the Junior Council, for which I have been forever grateful. The MOMA readings were on three Thursdays. The first was on April 26th with George Economou, Robert Kelly, and Armand Schwerner, introduced by Rochelle Owens. George and Armand were solid and in control. Kelly was more involved with the non-phenomenal world. The second was on May 3rd with John Giorno, Bernadette Mayer, and John Perreault, with Anne Waldman doing the introductions. John Giorno gave a fabulous performance full of his extraordinary energy. Bernadette read her difficult poetry quietly. John Perreault was beginning to experiment with performance art. The third was on May 10th with Kenward Elmslie, Barbara Guest, and Kenneth Koch, introduced by John Ashbery. It was a celebration of the New York School. After that we gave a reception in the Trustees Room.

On June 3, 1973, John Giorno, Anne Waldman and Michael Brownstein came to the country. We all swam in the pool and had lunch on the terrace. John had recovered completely from his cancer operation. He had had cancer in his left ball, which was removed. He was about to leave for Darjeeling, India, to visit His Holiness Dudjom Rinpoche, who was his Tibetan Buddhist guru.

In that year I published *Fever Coast* by Carter Ratcliff, now known chiefly as a distinguished art critic. The cover is a photograph of Carter. He is concerned with the nature of reality and man's destiny, which can only be approached through metaphor. As he says, in "Bacchus In Thebes," neither cleverness nor finesse can unravel the mystery. This, of course, suggests the influence of John Ashbery. We find another echo of Ashbery in those long sentences, which manage to maintain a logical syntax, though nearly swamped by the accumulating images. The inevitability of death is gently alluded to in "Los Grateful Muertos" and "Jack Frost Paints the Trees." Carter's involvement in art is made explicit in "Caravaggio Studies," though this poem is also about mortality, as the words "fever" and "feverish" suggest. "Fever," of course, may also refer to passion. As one can see, Ratcliff reveals himself as a very serious and ambitious writer in this book, and these qualities have been carried over into his art criticism. In 1973, I also published *In Baltic Circles* by Paul Violi. In the next year, Paul was to be appointed Poetry Chairman by the Junior Council; and I worked with him for many years in perfect harmony. The cover of *In Baltic Circles* is a painting of Paul by Paula North; he is very handsome. In an introduction to Paul reading at the museum, I once said, at a later date, that he was a "comic fantasist." In this, his first book, the phrase is less applicable. "Excerpts From The Chronicles" anticipates, perhaps, his later work. This is true of "Extract" as well; but the leaps in the narrative are not quite as broad as later came to be the case. "Summer" and "On The Rise" are straightforward accounts of the life around him, but many other poems have exotic settings. A voyage to distant places is an important theme. Straightfaced takeoffs on contemporary foolishness are also present. "Important Repercussions," among many other poems, reveals the acknowledged influence of Tony Towle. The dream as voyage, such as "Fever and Chills", is a common motif. The sharp accuracy of purely imaginative description is striking. Paul, though related to the New York School to some extent, cannot really be characterized as belonging to any particular group.

CHAPTER V

1974–1977

On Thursday, February 21, 1974, on the insistence of John Giorno and Anne Waldman, I began keeping a diary. We had been having lunch together at La Caravelle when they told me I must write my memoirs some day. I had never previously thought myself important enough to write my memoirs, but I took their advice. Therefore, this account of my life will be much fuller from 1974 on than it was for the previous years. The first entry tells of a dinner party I gave for the Schwartzes, the Violis, John Myers and Alexandra Anderson, a socialite who later became a serious art critic. John was very amusing and did an act imitating famous painters. He drew big yaks from Ally, who was a great fan of his. On the next day, I had lunch at La Caravelle with Morty, Martin Myerson, then the president of the University of Pennsylvania, and Craig Sweeten, the director of development, to discuss the plans for a contemporary art museum that never got built. That evening, I finished Allen Ginsberg's *Improvised Poetics*, which I found very lucid. Later in the month, I had lunch with Morty, Blake and one of Blake's friends. After having done brilliantly at Lawrenceville, he was then at the University of Pennsylvania, Morty's Alma Mater. We afterwards all went to the Metropolitan Museum to see the great medieval tapestry show. There I saw the marvelous apocalypse tapestries which I had first seen in the castle of Angers. A few days later, I conferred with my printer, Harry Gantt, about Larry Fagin's book, *Rhymes of a Jerk*, with a cover by Ed Ruscha, which almost didn't come out on time because Gantt lost the color transparency. Gantt, whom I inherited from Marc Schliefer, had always been my cross. He was never very bright; but, by this time, he was becoming both senile and blind. Ed Ruscha, who was hopping mad, provided us with an-

65

other transparency. On the 27th, I was in the country and supervised the rehanging of our Red Grooms after the living room was painted. The Grooms painting, *Picasso In Braque's Studio in 1913*, is a masterpiece. It is the most important painting we acquired in the early 70's. Also notable for that time is a nude in a landscape by Neil Welliver.

Early in March, I worked on Larry's proofs and conferred often with Gantt. I also went often to galleries and to the MOMA, where I approved the announcement for the April poetry readings. The design department of the museum made beautiful announcements, as always. I very much enjoyed working with the multi-talented Pat Whitman, the director of the Junior Council, now the Contemporary Arts Council. Pat and I soon became good friends. On the 19th, I had lunch at La Caravelle with Herb and John, who were their usual outrageous selves. Toward the end of the month, I gave a dinner party for the Pilgrims, then curators at the Brooklyn museum, Herb Machiz, art dealers Marilyn Fischbach and Paula Cooper and John Giorno. It was very successful. On the 29th, Morty and I went down to Philadelphia for an Institute of Contemporary Art weekend at Penn. We stayed at Janet Kardon's new house on the main line, which was out of this world, and, after dinner, went to a Phil Glass concert. Janet, at this point of her career, was the chairman of the I.C.A., not yet the director. The next day we had lunch at the University Museum, went over to see the Robert Morris show and then went back to the museum. The program there consisted of a lecture on time/space, by Dore Schary, and a round table discussion by Alan Kaprow, Phil Glass, Agnes Martin, Claes Oldenburg and Yvonne Rainer. That evening, I accepted Janet's invitation to be on the board of the I.C.A.

In early April, I interviewed Rochelle and took notes on her poems for the essay I was planning to write on her. On the 4th, the first poetry reading of the season took place, with Tony Towle, Larry Fagin and Michael Brownstein reading and Bernadette Mayer doing the introductions. There Larry approved the cover for his book; and afterwards, we took the poets to Lutece for dinner. The next day, Morty, Louis and I went to the pop art show at the Whitney. It looked very contemporary. On the 6th, we bought an Yvonne Jacquette, at Fischbach, and two Brainards. A few days later, we heard Barbara Guest read at the Donnell Library; and I began to take notes on Rochelle's plays. The second poetry reading of the season took place on the

11th, with Ted Greenwald, Paul Violi and Peter Schjeldahl reading and John Giorno doing the introductions. John also announced Peter's forthcoming marriage, followed by a list of the names of women Peter had made it with, who would miss him. Peter was furious at John. The evening was a smashing success. Afterwards, we took the poets to dinner at the Madrigal. The next day, my essay on John Giorno came out in *The Small Press Review*. I continued to take notes on Rochelle's plays; and, in the middle of the month, we bought a Robert Mangold at the Weber Gallery. The third and last poetry reading of the spring season took place on the 18th, with Ron Padgett, Dick Gallup and John Ashbery reading, and Barbara Guest doing the introductions. It was more sober than the previous readings but drew an enthusiastic crowd. A reception in the museum's Founder's Room followed. The next day we heard Rochelle read at the Women's Inter Art Center and went to one of Morris Golde's parties. I have never been able to figure out what Morris' function was in the poetry world, but he gave great parties. At this one, Rudy Burckhardt and James Schuyler praised my essay on Ashbery, which had just come out in *The World*. Throughout the month, I continued taking notes on Rochelle; and, on the 23rd, we had dinner at John and Herb's. Lee Krasner, Pollock's widow, and Ally were there; and the food and conversation were as super as ever. A few days later, I went to Kenward's play, "City Junket." The cast included Kenward, Irma Towle, Anne, Peter Schjeldahl, Clarice Rivers, Joe Brainard and John Ashbery. It was very pleasant. On the 26th, we went to the Schwartzes for dinner. The painter Natvar Bhavsar and Buffie Johnson were there, among others. Finally, on the 29th, Larry's publication party took place at the Gotham, at which John Ashbery told me he was pleased with my essay on him. Afterwards, we took Larry and Joan to San Marco for dinner.

To discuss the contents of *Rhymes of a Jerk*, Larry Fagin is, or was, a quintessential second generation, New York School, Saint Mark's Poetry Project person. I do not mean this as a denigration. I am supportive of the Poetry Project, and I am proud of Larry's book. It opens with twelve provocative short poems, followed by "Shaving in Paris," an I do this, I do that poem. "The Joke" is an uncool attack on his adulterous wife, while "Our Crowd" is a super cool list of New York Jews who write. Short poems follow that tease at glimmers of meaning. An untitled prose poem about a wall is very beautiful. Then there follow a group of poems, including the title poem, in which free association may be based on almost anything, including rhyme. "The Shore," with its repetition with variation , may be a comment, in its blankness, on many other poems. "Poems (1970)" gets closer to subject matter than the previous group and closes the first section of the book. The translations and collaborations that follow differ little in style from straight Larry Fagin.

On May 5th, the I.C.A. came to tour our country house and sculpture garden. We served them a buffet lunch and then drove up to the Storm King sculpture park with the Kardons. The landscaping at Storm King was beautiful, but the sculpture was of uneven quality. A couple of evenings later, we went to the Feather Ball with Alexander Liberman, painter, sculptor and editorial director of all Condé Nast publications. Andy Warhol was there and told his friends about my literary activities. The next evening we went to the Whitney Gala, which was a brawl. Throughout the month I worked on my essay on Rochelle, interrupted by my many other activities. On the 13th, Richard Kostelanetz came over with the manuscript of his book *I Articulations*, visual poems and fictions. Present at Buffie Johnson's cocktail party a few days later were the Schwartzes, Natvar Bhavsar and art dealers Max Hutchinson and Virginia Dwan. The next evening, the Kardons came up to the country and stayed overnight, after which we all drove up to the Libermans' house in Connecticut for lunch the next day. Alexander's new sculptures were fantastic. Lastly, at the end of the month, we brought Larry up to the country for the weekend.

On June 2nd, John and Herb gave us our twenty-fifth anniversary party at their house in Brewster. They decorated the table fabulously in silver and invited the Schwartzes to join us. Louis and Blake were also present. John and Herb were in their hilarious best form. On the 10th, I went to Philadelphia for my first I.C.A. meeting. I discovered that Susan Delehanty, the director, ran the whole show. The women on the board discussed parties, while the men discussed the budget. The fact that Blake was at Penn, and joined me for dinner afterwards, made these trips to Philadephia worthwhile for me. In the middle of the month we brought Herb and John up to the country for the weekend, where one night Herb cooked magnificently for us. Lotte Lenye came to dinner. She was a most fascinating woman, with the energy and sparkle of a much younger person. She would only sing when she got paid. Tough, selfish and stingy, she never reciprocated; but we loved her. She was a very wealthy woman but would keep no help, even in her eighties. Leo DuFour, our chauffer/chef at that time, liked to sing, play the harmonica and the tambourine, and dance for company. Lenye said, "Oh Morty, he is bad he is vunderfull." On the 22nd, we flew to Lisbon. It was a night flight, so we were very tired the next day and only got up to go out to dinner. We were very frustrated, because all the museums were closed, leaving us nothing interesting to do in Lisbon. A few days later, we drove to the Algarve and found it disappointing. On the 30th we flew to the French Riviera, where, at the wonderful hotel, La Reserve de Beaulieu, we had a very good time. On July 10th, we flew to Paris, where we went to the Louvre, the Miro exhibit at the Grande Palais and also paid our annual visit to the always gorgeous Notre Dame. On the 13th, we flew home. Soon after our arrival, I spent three hours in the Metropolitan Museum. It was my custom to substitute museums for galleries in the summer. Throughout the month I worked with Gantt and Kostelanetz and also read some of Charles Plymell's manuscript. On the 26th we drove up to the country with Gerard and his current girl friend, where I interviewed him for the essay I was about to write.

In August, I started taking notes on Gerard's poems, begininning with *Screen Tests*, and afterwards, *Chic Death*. On the 7th, Richard Serra came up to the country to pick a site for his maze-like structure in corten steel. One has a feeling of mystery walking through it. Before this, we had acquired Ronald Bladen's black inverted triangle, Alexander Liberman's large red sculpture, *Tropic*, a ninety-six foot wide bridge by Robert Grovesnor, in corten, and giant steel heads of us by Alex Katz. Serra was the most temperamental of the sculptors. He was very arrogant, and loved to play the old game of "épater le bourgeois." Rochelle and George came up to the country on the 17th and the Schwartzes later in the month. In the mean time, I took notes on Gerard's *Incarnations* and began writing the essay.

On Sept. 1st, John Cage, Merce Cunningham and Lenye came to lunch in the country; it was very gay. Meanwhile, I finished my essay on Gerard, and read manuscripts by Lewis Warsh and Tom Clark. In the middle of the month, Carter Ratcliff and Phyllis Derfner came up to the country for the weekend.

On October 1st, I went down to Soho, for the first time that season, and talked with Tony Towle, Paul Violi, Phil Glass, Richard Serra, Janet Kardon and Leo Castelli. Serra told me he was trying to start the foundation for our sculpture but the contractor was holding up the job. On the 3rd, we went to a cocktail party given by Cy Newhouse, in honor of Alexander Liberman. He has a fabulous town house and a fabulous collection. A couple of days later we went to the opening of Liberman's circle paintings from the 50's. They are gorgeous! He anticipated all the hard edge abstractions of the 60's. A little later on, I went to Charlemagne Palestine's studio to hear his music and engaged him for our November party. On the 9th, I went to Philadelphia for an I.C.A. meeting, some of which was interesting and some boring. Wanting to make myself useful, I suggested putting on a poetry reading for the 1975-1976 season. The committee was interested. The next day, we went to Al Held's smashing opening and out to dinner with the Kardons. In the middle of the month, the art movers, Lebron Brothers, came over to move our paintings; since we were in the process of having our apartment painted. They had to move them three times before the project was completed. In the mean time, I had a meeting with Barbara Jacobson, Ally and Paul to discuss the spring's poetry readings. On the 24th, the Gotham party for Richard Kostelanetz's book *I Articulations* took place. I was not as enthused about these visual poems and fictions as I was about most of my other books. Nevertheless, it represented an important aspect of avant garde literature at the time and was also related to the conceptual art then flooding the galleries. I always thought *Kulchur* should represent important current trends rather than my own taste exclusively. This tolerance was never extended to academic poetry.

Early in November, we had dinner at the Schwartzes. As usual, we admired their new acquisitions and enjoyed a gourmet dinner. Later in the month, we went to Neil Welliver's opening at Fischbach and then to Lil Picard's seventy-fifth birthday party. Lil was part of the same scene as Lenye in prewar Germany. On November 17th, Morty's birthday, the I.C.A. came to tour our apartment and, on the 21st, our annual big party took place. By this time, instead of entertaining a hundred guests, we had begun to receive almost two hundred. I still had to invite my old friends, while new generations of poets arrived on the horizon. The crashers were horrendous. As always, I served not only cocktails and hors d'oevers but a lavish buffet supper. As

Morty patrolled the apartment to protect it from damage, the parties were beginning to get tiresome, for us if not for the guests. Later in the month, we went to another big bash, the Kardons' twenty-fifth anniversary party. Finally, at the end of the month, John Giorno brought over Charles Plymell's manuscript, which he had edited, and the Les Levine cover. I spent several days going over this material.

On Dec. 5th, 1974, I went to John Giorno's loft at 222 Bowery for lunch, for the first time. It was delicious; John is a gourmet cook. Gantt and Les Levine were there to go over both the manuscript and the cover for Charles Plymell's book, and to pick the type. Though a very good poet, Plymell was incapable of organizing his own work. A few days later we went to the Schwartzes' for dinner, where Herb and John were as witty and outrageous as ever. On the 11th, I went to Philadelphia for an I.C.A. meeting, at which the poetry reading I was to arrange was scheduled for the following September. On the 17th, I interviewed Anne Waldman in preparation for writing about her; and, on the same day, I had a meeting with Paul and Ally to discuss the spring poetry readings. At the end of the month, we celebrated New Year's Eve with a party at our country house.

On New Years Day, 1975, the painter Richard Pousette Dart and his wife Evelyn, neighbors of ours in the country, came over for cocktails. On the 5th, we flew to London, where we saw the great Turner show at the Royal Academy. On the 8th, we flew to ugly Frankfurt for the textile show Morty was obliged to revisit every year and, on the 10th, to beautiful Munich. In Munich, we went to the super Pinopoteke Museum, to a lovely seventeenth century baroque church and to a medieval church which, unfortunately, was all restored. On the 13th, we flew to Vienna and visited the art museum with its beautiful nineteenth century interior. On the 16th, we flew to Paris, where I ordered my dress for Louis' wedding at Nina Ricci, visited the Louvre and Notre Dame, and finally, flew home on the 19th. A couple of days later Gantt came over with the proofs of Plymell's *The Trashing of America*, and, a few days after that, brought me the cover proof. On the 29th, I started taking notes on Anne's *No Hassles* and, on the next evening, I gave a dinner party for Herb and John, Lenye, the art dealer Klaus Kertiss and the Violis.

On Feb. 5th, I collated my proofs with Pam Plymell's, who was doing Charles' proofreading for him. A couple of days later I went to the

Whitney Biennial and found it awful. That evening, I started taking notes on Anne's *Giant Night*. On the 11th, I had lunch with John Myers, whose gallery was still surviving; though his break with Tibor was the great mistake of his life. Later that day, Susan Delehanty came over to discuss the poetry reading to take place at Penn in September; and, in the evening, Anne Waldman and Michael Brownstein came to dinner. At a studio performance of the Merce Cunningham company on the 15th, the music of Meredith Monk impressed me very much. The next day, I started reading Tom Clark's manuscript, *At Malibu*. A couple of days later, I went to the superb Max Ernst show at the Guggenheim and, in the evening, went to hear the great but psychotic poet, John Wieners, read at the Donnell Library. I was relieved that he read well, because I realized I was taking a big risk in planning to have him read at the MOMA in the spring. My next task that month was taking notes on Anne's *Baby Breakdown* and *Life Notes*. Toward the end of the month, we went to dinner at the Pousette Darts', and finally, on the 27th, I gave a dinner party for the Myersons, the Schwartzes and Leo Castelli.

On March 6th, we went to dinner at John and Herb's. Ally was there and Adolph Gottlieb's widow. I bought a small Goodnough from John who had finally been forced to close his gallery. Between the 9th and the 18th we were in California, and on the 21st, we went to a party given by Andrew Wylie for Gerard's birthday. Present were Anne and Michael, Lewis Warsh, then engaged to Bernadette Mayer, and Armand Schwerner, recently separated from his wife, Dolores. On the 25th, I had lunch with John Giorno at the Spring Street Bar and, on the next day, began taking notes on Anne's great long poem, "Fast Speaking Woman." Toward the end of the month, we went to see Rochelle's play, "He Wants Shih," which I felt had a poor production; and, a couple of days later, a professor from the Harvard department of Architecture came down to see our house.

On April 2nd, I started writing my essay on Anne and, on the next day, met with Leo Castelli to discuss plans for the party celebrating the installation of our Serra sculpture. On the 7th the first poetry reading of the season took place at the MOMA. It was a smash hit and drew a large and very responsive audience. George Economou introduced John Wieners, Charles Reznikoff and Jerome Rothenberg. At intermissions I padded after Wieners to make sure he didn't get into trouble. He was shy but in control. Reznikoff was gentleness and clarity itself, while Jerry brought down the house with his very funny American Indian translations. After the reading, we went out to dinner with Rochelle and George; and, on the next day, my essay on Gerard came out in the *Small Press Review*. The day after, I went to an I.C.A. meeting, where the September poetry reading was formally approved. On the 11th, we went to the Guggenheim to see the great Brice Marden show. I very much regret not having acquired one of his paintings before the prices got too high. On the 14th, the second poetry reading of the season took place at the MOMA. Paul Violi introduced the sensational Helen Adam, one of my very favorite poets, the equally sensational Anne Waldman, reading from "Fast Speaking Woman," and Rebecca Wright, who was dull. On the 21st, the third and last poetry reading of the season took place at the MOMA. Larry Fagin introduced Lewis MacAdams, Carter Ratcliff and David Meltzer. It was the weakest of the three readings; they were all good poets but poor readers. A few days later, I gave a dinner party for the Fagins, the Ratcliffs, and Barbara Jacobson. Finally, on the 28th, the Gotham Book Mart party for *The Trashing of America* took place. Charles Plymell proved to be a good poet but a creep. At dinner afterwards, he got very drunk and began to call Allen Ginsberg, who had recommended his work to me, a kike. If he had not been a poet, I would have had him thrown out of the restaurant.

The Trashing of America is a strong book in what may be loosely called the beat tradition. Les Levine's cover is a quite literal interpretation of the title. It shows a heap of trash, on top of which is a television set with Nixon's face on the screen. The first poem, beginning with the line, "Bend down America and kiss the concrete," is bitter about the absolute boredom the poet feels in confronting our society. It is not at all an original sentiment, but Plymell lends passion to it. Scenes of the Bowery, the infuriating sameness of everything, some effective obscenity, "opportunist, sycophant, suck ass," continue in the poems; while "bend down and kiss the concrete" becomes a repeated refrain. "Throw Down the Key" is a magnificent poem in which the repulsive suburbanites are contrasted with holy bums. Plymell's music is powerful. Contamination is everywhere. The dead serpent and caged tiger symbolize our guilt. The poem ends with "Julius Caesar! Hamlet! Robin Hood!" In another poem, the drowned Hart Crane lies at the feet of the Statue of Liberty. "A Forgotten Filling Station in Kansas" reminds one of Hopper. Scenes of New York give way to the road and other cities. Incantatory rhythms persist. A dead pigeon joins the serpent and tiger in the catalogue of martyrs. Allen Ginsberg, Neal Cassady and Pound are invoked. In another poem his brother, his mother and his childhood stop short of sentimentality; the emotion is too sincere for sentiment. Hollywood as hell is another unoriginal theme which Plymell makes ring true through the force of his feeling. A visit to Burroughs in London and to revolution torn Paris extends his beat voyage. "Star Tattoo Dying On the Day-Glow Ganges" reaches a peak of passionate invocation. There follow the poems of martyrdom: "Christ Is Alive In A Bum Sleeping In His Piss On A Sidewalk," "Christ Is Alive In A Tiger In The Central Park Zoo," "Christ Is Alive In The Alley Of Mud," "Christ Is Alive In A Mongoloid Child Who." The long poem "Glory Revolution--1963" sums up Plymell's themes. The book closes with photographs of the author at various stages of his life, and villainous Nixon reappears on the back cover.

On May 4th, the party in honor of our Serra sculpture took place at our country house. It was a super party, including many museum people. Serra, quite typically, didn't show up. On the 7th, we went to dinner at Tom Armstrong's, the director of the Whitney, and, afterwards, to the Whitney Gala. A couple of days later, we flew to London and then on to Paris where we went for the express purpose of fitting my dress for Louis' wedding and bringing it back to New York. Louis, who was always a gorgeous child, had grown up very handsome and, after graduation from Penn, had joined Morty's business. He was engaged to a beautiful girl named Wendy Mann, whom he had courted for six years. She was from a prominent Philadelphia family. I bought a fabulous hat for the wedding at Nina Ricci, which they packed in a huge box stuffed with tissue paper. Naturally, I couldn't check it aboard with the luggage. Therefore, when we arrived at the gate, we were told the box was too big to carry aboard the aircraft. I insisted it *had* to go aboard, because it was for my son's wedding. After much altercation, the supervisor told us we could carry the box aboard if we put a seat belt around it. Therefore, we bought a seat for the hat and brought it to New York. When we got home, I had a conference with

Bernadette Mayer about her book, *Poetry*. She was pregnant and told me she might marry Lewis Warsh. At the end of the month, we drove John and Herb up to the country for the weekend, where Herb was very depressed about his career.

On June 1st, Lotte Lenye came for lunch, which was very gay; and Herb got over his depression. Afterwards, we went over to Lenye's house for cocktails, Throughout the month, I was busy with the proofs of Tom Clark's book, *At Malibu*. On the 10th, we went to the Party in the Garden at the MOMA. This has always been the high point of my social year, for which I wear my best gowns and jewelry. On the 19th, Gerard came over to take photographs of Louis, Blake, Morty and me in order to memorialize the family as it had been, just before Louis' wedding. The next day we took Helen Adam to the country for the weekend. Helen, a genuine witch, who believes passionately in the supernatural, was enchanting, collecting "mysterious rocks," which she believed to be living beings, and telling our fortunes with the Tarot cards. She frightened our couple, Leo and Yvonne, who asked if her magic was "blanc ou noir." Morty told them "noir." Finally, on June 29th, Louis and Wendy got married. It was a beautiful wedding, at the reformed Temple in Philadelphia. The reception was at the Berkeley Hotel. I did not cry at the wedding like most Jewish mothers, who feed on their sons. I was so happy for Louis that the wedding pictures show me grinning like a fool.

On July 3rd, we flew to London and then on to Venice. There, we visited, once again, the usual great sights; for we had been in Venice many times before. On the 11th, we flew to Rome, from there to Nice and from there to glorious La Reserve de Beaulieu. After a wonderful time swimming and sunbathing, we flew to Paris on the 20th. There, we took a day trip to see Chartres, once again, and then flew home on the 23rd. At the end of the month, we went to visit John and Herb at their house in Brewster. They had become two bitter old men, whose careers were over, and had lost most of their spark. On August 2nd, the Schwartzes came up to our country house for the weekend, where we gave a dinner party for them and some neighbors on Saturday night. Back in New York, we went to the birthday party of Diane Costello, Gerard's girl friend at the time, where I chatted with David Ignatow and Taylor Mead.

On Sept. 6th, 1975, John Giorno and the Levines came up to the country for the weekend. Les spent most of his time watching T.V. John, by this time one of my best friends, joined Les in telling me the art and literature of the past did not matter. I was not at all convinced, though I listened politely. On the 9th, I started taking notes on Diane Wakoski's poems, in preparation for writing an essay on her. The next evening, we went to a party at the Castelli gallery in honor of Andy's new book *The Philosophy of Andy Warhol*. Back in the country again, the Violis came to lunch; and Paul and I discussed the next season's poetry readings. On the 27th, Jay Clayton played tapes for us, and we hired her music ensemble to play for us at our annual big party. On the 30th, I put a reserve on a Brad Davis painting at the new Holly Solomon Gallery in Soho. Holly, whom I had met through the Schwartzes several years earlier, was a leading collector of Pop Art in the sixties, when she had been an aspiring actress. Later on, though not yet a professional dealer, she opened the now famous 98 Greene St. loft, where she put on art shows and also plays, in which she herself acted. In 1975, having given up her ambitions in the theatre, she opened her gallery, where she pioneered in the pattern and decoration movement. When I saw the brilliantly decorative Brad Davis paintings at her first show, after years of looking at minimal and conceptual art, I felt like I had received a shot in the arm.

On Oct. 4th, I brought Morty to Holly's gallery and finalized the acquisition of the Brad Davis "Black Orchid." A few days later, I started writing my essay on Diane Wakoski. I had lunch with John and Herb once again on the 14th. They were no longer entertaining, but I remained loyal to them of course. On the 16th I went to an I.C.A. meeting and, on the 23rd, my first poetry reading at Penn took place. Larry Fagin introduced Gerard Malanga, John Giorno and Anne Waldman. It was super, and we had a great audience response. Finally, on the 27th, the Gotham Book Mart party for Tom Clark's *At Malibu* took place.

In the language of the vernacular, wittily exaggerated, Tom Clark reveals the hopelessness of contemporary society; but this is no dull social realist book. In racy, swiftly moving images Clark presents the funny and the disgusting. The cover photograph shows Tom naked; but his penis is not visible, because his legs are crossed. "One More Saturday Night" reveals the sensitivity, which gives rise to his indignation. "Goodbye" reveals the poetic fire which is scraped up out of nothingness. Playing baskeball provides relief. "You Make The Connections" coolly presents the horrors of everyday life. The wonderful long poem "Chicago" describes his experience as an usher at public events at age 15. Sports, first introduced into literature by Jack Kerouac, play a large part in Tom's poems. His erotic fantasy in "United Flight 127" is a masterpiece. Fantasy plays a part in three more poems, followed by the straight faced comedy of "Niné Songs." Section II of the book, "Hand Jive," opens with a series of one line poems followed by "Suite," a series of romantic poems which show the other side of Clark's poetic persona. A great many love poems follow, then "Japan," a philosophical poem addressed to Reverdi, and finally, "Death Soup," cool three line stanzas which revert to Clark's attack on society. *At Mailbu* is a superb and many sided book.

After spending the first week of November in California, on the 11th we went to the ballet. We enjoyed it, though it was not as great at Lincoln Center as it has been at the City Center. The next day we went to the DiSuvero opening at the Whitney, which was an awful mob scene. On the 20th, our annual big party took place. Soon after this, I went through Bernadette Mayer's manuscript, *Poetry*, and worked on it the rest of the month. On Dec. 3rd, I started my essay on *Kulchur* magazine, commissioned by Triquarterly, and continued work on it throughout the month. On the 16th, I had lunch with Rochelle and bought three Brainards at Fischbach. A few days later, my essay on Ed Dorn appeared in the Shore Review. Still later in the month, we went to a cocktail party at Lotte Lenye's and also saw the fabulous Red Grooms environment, "Ruckus Manhattan." Finally, on the 31st, we gave a New Year's Eve party for Herb and John, Lenye and other neighbors in the country.

On New Year's Day, 1976, we went to a party at Jane Freilicher's with Herb and John. There we learned from Jane's husband, Joe Hazan, that John originally wanted to be a modern dancer when he first came to New York. Never having known John young and slim, it struck me funny. On the 11th, we flew to London and then on to awful Frankfurt. On the 17th, we flew to Milan and then drove to beautiful Florence, where we had been many times before though never before in the winter. We took a day trip to Siena to see the adorable cathedral once again and the great Duccios. We found the Uffizzi

Gallery more overwhelming than ever. On the 21st, we drove to Rome and flew from there to Paris. The next day, in the city of light, we had lunch with John Giorno, the French poet Bernard Heidsieck and his wife Francoise, and poet/novelist/painter Brion Gysin. The lunch was at Vivarois and we had great oysters and lobster. On January 24th, we went to John Giorno's performance, at a Poesie Sonore Festival organized by Bernard, and, at that time, a totally new kind of event in Paris. The next day, we had Moroccan tea at Brion Gysin's, who was recovering from colon cancer. That evening we all had cocktails with the Heidsiecks in their fabulous 17th Century apartment on the Ile Saint Louis. On the 26th, we flew home.

On Feb. 5th, my essay on Rochelle came out in *Margins*, and I finished working on Bernadette's proofs. The next day, I wrote my Introduction to *Kulchur Queen*, my collected essays to be published by Giorno Poetry Systems. Later in the month we went to a party at Holly's gallery, and a few days later, I went to an I.C.A. meeting in Philadelphia. At the end of the month, we had dinner at John and Herb's. On March 12th, we had dinner at the Schwartzes' and saw the Solomons and the Kardons there. As always, we had a very good time. The next day, we went to a party at Les Levine's. John Giorno, John Perreault, Carter Ratcliff and the art critic, Grace Glueck, were present. As may be expected, it was a lot of fun. On the 18th, I gave a dinner party for John and Herb, the Violis, Lenye and Lenye's friend, Margo. John Myers, who had become more and more arrogant and vicious, attacked Morty about a book John loved and Morty found boring. I sprang to Morty's defense and let John have it. Sour and angry at the world, John was beginning to get on my nerves. On the last week of the month, we took our usual spring trip to California.

On April 4th, we had dinner at Helen Adam's. She has a tiny, tiny apartment filled with books and pictures. There is much of the occult on display. She was trying to get us to take a one eyed cat, whom she said spoke to her and asked her to find him a home. On the next day, the first of my poetry readings of the season took place at the MOMA. Harvey Shapiro introduced Rochelle Owens, David Ignatow and Jackson MacLow. Rochelle was her usual vivid and eccentric self, Ignatow was straighforward and strong and MacLow proved that he had anticipated the avant garde by twenty years. The next day,

I had lunch with John Myers and Herb Machiz, to whom I was still loyal; and, the day after that, I went to an I.C.A. meeting. On the following day, I went to Les Levine's studio to be photographed for the covers of *Kulchur Queen*. Afterwards, I had lunch at the Grotta Azzurra with Les and John Giorno. There John gave the book its title, *Kulchur Queen*, which at first I objected to; but he didn't have much trouble talking me into it. On the 12th, the second poetry reading of the season took place at the MOMA, with Charles North, Maureen Owen and Gerard Malanga. Charles was weak, Maureen was very good and Gerard had developed and deepened considerably. On the 17th, Les came over to show Morty and me proofs of the cover pictures for *Kulchur Queen*. On that occasion, he asked Morty if he had any more pictures of me. Morty replied with an enthusiastic yes, so Les went home with a lot of glamorous photographs taken when I was young. At first I thought them inappropriate for a book of literary criticism, but soon I began to like the idea. On the same day I went to the office to look at our newly acquired Wofford, and then Morty and I went over to Tibor DeNagy and bought an Ian Hornak. On the 19th, the third poetry reading of the season took place. It was an evening of artists who write. It included Claes Oldenburg, Joe Brainard and Larry Rivers and was a smashing success. Oldenburg was only fair, Joe was very good and Larry, who read from his autobiography, was hilarious. He said, upon being invited to the White House, that they shouldn't have invited him because he was a cocksucker and a muff diver. On the 22nd, we went to the Solomon's for dinner. Ted Greenwald, then editor of the St. Mark's Newsletter, took my essay on Anne Waldman for consideration. On May 3rd, I presided over the Gotham Book Mart party for Bernadette's, *Poetry*. It was a poor turnout, because Bernadette was not there. She had a four month old infant and was still nursing.

Poetry is a book in which some poems are built upon the multiple uses of words rather than upon the related meanings of words. The cover drawing is by Bernadette's sister, Rosemary. The first poem is about the word "corn." This method is carried over to the next poem, where there is a play on names beginning with the letter J. There follows a poem built on "three men," "girls," "a man," "a boy," "coat," "box," "boat" and "a lighthouse." Meanings are discontinuous. This is related to language poetry. "Anthology," a long work, is based on flowers, medical abbreviations, crimes, bridges, high peaks, salutations, maximum penalties for first degree murder, crops gestation and incubation periods, coffee, grain products, causes of fires, anti-popes, dogs, disasters, crude and inedible material, occupations, horses, the Circus Hall of Fame, comets, flowers, the Hohenstaufens, money winning horses, types of households, embellishments on U.S. currency backs, lamp inventions, Atlantic islands, heads of state, figures in the life of Abraham Lincoln, marine disasters, gases, metals, nonmetals, American cars, state nicknames, occupation groups, units of length, U.S. Army noncommissioned officers' chevrons, salt water fish, time, seven wonders of the world, salutes, burned buildings, ancient plants and animals and trees. Poems follow which contain a play of actions surrounding one word and poems in which the method of association is obscure. However, the latter don't appear to be built on rapid free association, as in *Album* or *Bean Spasms*, but on something more calculated and cerebral. The kinds of poems in this book characterize Bernadette's early work and that associated with Vito Acconci and his magazine *0 to 9*. Later on she was to develop a much simpler and more personal style.

From the 1st of May until the 9th, I worked on Sotère Torregian's manuscript, *The Age of Gold*. A couple of days later, I went to Holly's gallery and bought a Brad David pastel for Louis' first anniversary. John Giorno came to dinner that night, and, later, on the 21st, he and the Levines, came over and gave the manuscript of *Kulchur Queen* to Gantt. On the next day, I commissioned a section of Jennifer Bartlett's great painting, "Rhapsody," at the Paula Cooper gallery. "Rhapsody," an enormous work on the history of contemporary painting, covered all four walls of the gallery. Collectors could commission the reproduction of *one* section that could then not be reproduced by anyone else. We chose the abstract expressionist section, which was to be called "Big Trees." From that day until the 24th, I studied my letters from poets in order to send a selection to Mary Kinzie of Triquarterly to accompany my essay on *Kulchur* magazine in *The Little Magazine In America, A Documentary History*. Toward the end of the month, the Schwartzes came to the country for the weekend, and

I gave a dinner party for them and some of the neighbors. At the same time, my essay on Anne came out in the *Poetry Project Newsletter*.

On May 25, 1976, Bernard Heidsieck's wife, Francoise Janicot, then on a visit to New York, came to dinner with John Giorno. On June 5th, Francoise came to the country for the weekend. After attending a party at the Fischbach gallery, we returned to the country the next weekend with the Towles. Their little girl, Rachel, was then an exceptionally beautiful child. On the 16th, the Party in the Garden took place at the MOMA, before which we went to a dinner party at Judy Winslow's, the chairman of the Junior Council at that time. On the 19th, we flew to London with my mother as our guest. I did my best to show her the sights; but it was unusually hot in London, and she petered out at St. Paul's. On the 24th, we flew to Nice and on to La Reserve, where all of us had a wonderful time. On July 6th, we flew to Paris, where we had lunch with the Heidsiecks, and where I took my mother to the Louvre and Notre Dame. On the 12th, we flew home; and, on the next day, Gantt brought the proofs of both *The Age of Gold* and *Kulchur Queen*. A couple of days later, Stuart Lavin, Gerard's protegé, came over to meet me; and, a couple of days after that, the Violis came to lunch. The next weekend, the Solomon's came to the country, where Holly, like Les Levine and John Giorno, put down the art of the past. On the 28th, I paged up *Kulchur Queen* and collated Sotère's proofs with mine. On the 30th, we took the Greenwalds to the country for the weekend.

On the 3rd of August, I had lunch with Holly and selected a Brad Davis crayon drawing for my mother's birthday. On the 10th, the photographer, Bill Yoscary, came over with pictures taken at the Gotham Book Mart for *Kulchur Queen*. We also took a photograph of Andy Warhol's portrait of me. On the 27th, we received the shocking news from Lenye that Herb Machiz had died. On the 1st of September, we had dinner at the Schwartzes' with our children, where Wendy flipped for their apartment. In the middle of the month, I had lunch with John Myers who was grief stricken at Herb's death; although he had taken another lover, Arthur Cady, before Herb died. Toward the end of the month, I had lunch with Holly in Soho, and, on the 28th, went to Philadelphia for an I.C.A. meeting. On Oct. 1st, John Giorno came over to do the final work on *Kulchur Queen* before it went into page proof. On the 12th, I had lunch with Rochelle. On the 21st, Les and Cathy Levine came to dinner, and Les described the conceptual portrait he wished to do of me. A couple of days later, Sotère arrived from California so that he could be present at his publication party; and on the 25th, the party took place at the Gotham.

Sotère is a poet heavily influenced by classical surrealism, which *The Age of Gold* reflects. The cover is by Sotère himself and presents pictures of Marisol and André Breton. Most of the images of the title poem are cast in Italy; but Greek mythology, Egyptian sculpture, Viennese waltzes and American films also appear. "Is It For This I Live?" is a beautiful poem with the characteristically surrealist images of "infinite woman," "subaltern of desire," "tullieries of the Bronx Zoo," "the crushed eye of Babylon" and "a coin box in the shape of a lighthouse." "You Warned Against Those Modern Manichean Types" speaks of "the machine-gun of the Apocalypse," "the cults of Onan and Isis," "the highpriest's ear cut off" and "guillotined by my name." "Anya" is especially rich in these leaping images: "a big umbrella over the land tomorrow," "Trojan horse of exposed photographs," "pubescence gliding by on a bike," "clay pipes of the stars," "morning domed like a bird," "crushed tin plates of camp sites" and "hidden places of feces." It is the exotic nature of the imagery and the passionate tone which distinguishes *The Age of Gold* from New York School surrealism, and surely it is at the opposite pole from Bernadette's cerebral *Poetry*. This demonstrates the eclecticism of my taste, which is also revealed in my art collection.

From the 31st of October to Nov. 13th, we vacationed in California. On Nov. 16th, the musician, Jon Gibson, came to our apartment to inspect the space for playing at our annual big party; and, on the 18th, the party took place. On the 21st, along with most of the art world, we went to see Robert Wilson's opera (if so it can be called) "Einstein On The Beach," with music by Phil Glass. Christopher Knowles, "the idiot savant," wrote the text; and Lucinda Childs brilliantly danced the leading role. We thought it was great but couldn't sit through the whole thing. At the end of the month, I looked over Lewis MacAdams' manuscript, *Live At The Church*; and, on Dec. 4th, we went to the opening of the Kurt Weill/Lotte Lenye Museum at Lincoln Center. On the 9th, my second poetry reading at Penn took place. Michael Brownstein introduced Helen Adam, Paul Violi and Ron Padgett. Helen was sensational and Paul good; but Ron, though a very important poet, is a poor reader. A couple of days later, we had lunch at the Grotta Azzura with Paula Cooper and Jennifer Bartlett, and then went to Jennifer's studio to see our painting, which was gorgeous. Jennifer went out and bought a bottle of the powerful Italian brandy, Grappa, on which we all got loaded. On the same afternoon, we went to Holly's gallery to see the Brad Davis we had commissioned and to pick up our little Thomas Lanigan Schmidt icon. In the middle of the month I had lunch with Holly; and, a few days later, Helen came to dinner. She was shocked when I offered her $500.00 to do a book and said money was bad luck. She also gave me a beautiful agate necklace. On the 21st, I had lunch with Gerard; and, afterwards, Gantt came over with the blueprint of *Kulchur Queen*, which John Giorno came to look at the next day and pick paper samples. That night I went to a party at John Myers', which was depressing; and on the 29th, Horace Solomon came up to the country to hang the new Brad Davis. On Jan. 5, 1977, Paula and Jennifer came up to the country to hang "Big Trees." It was a very long and difficult job, because the painting is composed of many small metal plates. A couple of days later, we had dinner at Holly's, where we were joined by the Greenwalds and Brad Davis. From the 9th to the 24th, we were in Europe, during which time we went to Madrid just to see the Prado once more. On the 5th of February, I started work on Lewis MacAdams' proofs for *Live At The Church*. On the 8th, I interviewed Ted Berrigan for my essay on him; and, on the next day, my 50th birthday, the publication party for my second book, *Kulchur Queen*, took place at the Gotham. Unlike my first book *The Intricate Image*, it dealt with contemporary American literature. We had a large turnout at the party, and I was very happy. The front cover, by Les Levine, is a gorgeous photograph of me in full color, wearing a gold brocade ball gown by Nina Ricci and looking over a huge bouquet of red roses. The back cover, also by Les, is another photograph of me in the same dress. The book contains nine essays: an essay on *Kulchur* magazine, commissioned by *Triquarterly* for *The Little Magazine In America*, an essay on Dorothy Richardson, which was a digest of my master's thesis, commissioned by John Myers, and then not used in his magazine, *Parenthèse*, and essays on the poetry of John Ashbery, John Giorno, Ed Dorn, Rochelle Owens, Anne Waldman, Gerard Malanga and Diane Wakoski. On the next day, William Rubin, the curator of Painting and Sculpture at the MOMA, came over to see our collection; we had promised him the gift of some paintings for the museum. On the 17th, we bought a painting by Randy Stevens, a takeoff on a cheerleader, from the Kornblee gallery. Also on February 17th, 1977, we had dinner at Lutece with John Giorno and Francoise and Bernard Heidsieck. They were in from Paris for a show of Francoise's work at "C" Space on Leonard Street. On February 22, the Heidsiecks and John Giorno came to the country for dinner and spent the night.

In the beginning of March, I received a letter from LeRoi, signed Amiri Baraka, and strangely addressing me as Mrs. Hornick. Delighted to hear from him again after so many years, I called the number he gave; and he returned my call on March 8th. It seems he wanted some backing for his play, "The Progress of History." I arranged for him to come visit us on the 26th of the month. Before that time, we took a week's trip to California and also had Frances Waldman to dinner, who, generously lent me some books by Ted Berrigan. When LeRoi arrived, after our twelve year separation, we all hugged. He was soft spoken, charming, and didn't look much older. Morty and he discussed politics just like the old days. He said he was "an identified communist" and admired China and Albania but not Russia, which he called a capitalist country. He believed the U.S. and Russia were on the brink of World War III. After discussing the current poetry scene with him, I showed him my publications, and gave him inscribed copies of *The Intricate Image* and *Kulchur Queen*. We promised him a contribution for his play and told him we would come to the opening and take him out to dinner, after which we parted. At the end of the month, I went over the final proofs of *Live At The Church* and started writing on Ted.

On April 4th, 1977, my first poetry reading of the season took place at the MOMA. Barbara Guest introduced Ted Berrigan, Lewis Warsh and Bill Zavatsky. Ted was superb and both Lewis and Bill were very good; we had a full house. Irv Sandler complimented me on *Kulchur Queen*, while Shelly Lustig said she was trying to get permission to review it for the Times with no success. Shortly thereafter, I received a beautiful letter from Joe Brainard about it, with a drawing of me as a teddy bear. I also received a letter from Paul, and Ted said he loved it and was dying to see my essay on him. On the 11th, my second poetry reading of the season took place at the MOMA. Charles North introduced Joe Ceravolo, David Shapiro and Frank Lima. Joe read with lyric beauty, David was both funny and learned and Frank was very strong. Joe told me he had read *Kulchur Queen* from cover to cover and couldn't get over it. Afterwards we all went to a party at Christophe de Menil's, arranged by David. On the 18th, my third poetry reading of the season took place at the MOMA; it was another evening of artists who write. Larry Rivers, who sported a T-shirt saying "GAY IS GOOD," introduced Jennifer Bartlett, Jim Dine and Brigid Polk, who read from Warhol's writings. Jennifer implied a fear of living alone in a loft and a fear of rape, Jim Dine was excellent and Brigid, though very nervous, came through all right. On the 25th, the publication party for Lewis MacAdams' *Live At The Church* took place at the Gotham.

The cover of *Life At The Church* is a photograph of the author by Gerard Malanga. The poems are somewhat more easily available than many works of the St. Mark's Church persuasion; this is not to say that they are at all simplistic. "Joanne's Birthday," about the 40th birthday of Joanne Kyger, is a lovely and seemingly effortless example of MacAdams' manner. It is followed by an untitled poem about working in a barn, which is direct and refreshing. "Worlds In Love," a collaboration with Anne Waldman and Maureen Owen, has more rapid transitions, held together by the color "green." "To Phoebe This Morning" is surreal, while "To Phoebe Gone To Wendy" is a clear account of the pangs of love. "Swimming Along With The Tide" passes rapidly from image to image; but the subject, sexual love, is not obscured by such transitions. "Specimen Stairs," despite the title, is almost linear in its clarity, while the last poem, "Live At The Church" reaches great heights. On the whole, this book does not represent a markedly original personal style; but many styles, familiar in contemporary poetry, are handled competently.

On April 28th, 1977, Les Levine photographed John Giorno, Anne and me for the cover of a record album I co-sponsored with Giorno Poetry Systems. It is a double album featuring John on one record and Anne on the other. Les photographed us in Madison Square Park at Fifth Avenue and 23rd Street. I thought it best that I wear all black, with some of my gold jewelry. The front cover shows John and Anne walking in the park, front view, with me seated on a bench, front view, in color. The back cover, also in color, shows Anne and I walking in the park, back view, with John seated on a bench, front view. The inside cover, in black and white, shows very large heads of John and Anne with very serious expressions. Side I of John's record is entitled "Everyone Is A Complete Disappointment." In John's familiar manner, images of despair, pain, anxiety, terror, pleasure, sex, bliss, emptiness, Buddhism and the ephemera of our culture succeed each other rapidly. The title of Side II is "Drinking The Blood Of Every Woman's Period." *I loved it*! There is actually no drinking of menstrual blood in the poem. The title is wholly metaphorical, suggesting total degradation or uttermost abandonment, transformed into absolute purity. Side I of Anne's record contains seven short poems. Side II contains her great poem "Fast Speaking Woman," delivered in a magnificent incantatory style. Freedom and power is the theme.

On May 5th, we bought a Jack Youngerman sculpture at the Pace gallery. On the 10th, I had lunch with Frances Waldman and Holly. Holly came late and had only bourbon and soda. Her gallery was then at the height of its popularity. On the same afternoon, Gantt came over to go over the manuscript for Helen's book, *Turn Again To Me*. On the next day, we bought a section of the Katz macquette which was being used for a giant billboard on Times Square. This billboard was entirely composed of beautiful women's heads. The next day, I had lunch at Lutece with John Giorno, who told me he was having difficulty having another book published because all the poetry presses were run by coteries to which he did not belong. On the 14th, we had dinner at Lotte Lenye's, a unique occasion, since she never entertained. A few days later, we had dinner with the Solomons; and, on the 28th, the Schwartzes came up to the country with their son, Michael. That evening I gave a dinner party for them with the realist artist, Anne Poor, and Billie Harkavy, in her youth the leading designer of theatrical sets and costumes.

On June 14th, I met Brad Davis at the office to consult with him about his project to design a bedspread for Morty's Fall River factory.

A few days later we went to see LeRoi's play, "The Progress of History." It was written down to the level of the most uneducated blacks. We were the only white people in the theatre. A reading list of Marxist texts was passed out to all members of the audience. It began at 8 PM; and, at 11:40, we went out for a breath of air and were told that it would be over around midnight but that there would be a question and answer period afterwards. We went back and told LeRoi that we would have to postpone our dinner date, and went to the Grotta Azzurra for dinner ourselves. From June 19th to July 11th we were in Europe and, on the 17th, went to a party at the Schwartzes'. On the 23rd, Brad Davis and Ned Smythe came to the country for lunch. They were collaborating on a new show. Finally, on the 31st, the Violi's came for lunch; and Paul and I discussed the next season's poetry readings.

On Aug. 6th, John Myers and his new lover, Arthur Cady, came to the country for the weekend. Arthur had been married about thirty years and had had children and grandchildren before he came out of the closet. John was outrageously vicious, insulting Morty. Later, alone with me, he became lugubrious. On the next weekend, Holly and Horace came up to the country and Lenye came to dinner. That week I went up to Boston with Blake to furnish his apartment. He was about to enter Boston College Law School. I had invited John Wieners to have dinner with us in order to interview him. He didn't show up, but came for lunch the next day. He was evidently going through one of his more troubled periods, because he was quite incoherent during our interview. For the rest of the month, I took notes on his poetry. On Sept. 10th, we went to Brad and Ned's opening at Holly's. It was spectacular. Brad's paintings had become even more lush, containing birds and animals as well as foliage. Ned's sculptures, a great departure from primary structures, were based on Islamic architecture. Afterwards, we went to a party at Holly's. On the 13th, I discussed the next season's poetry readings with Paul, Gerritt Lansing, the new chairman of the Junior Council, and Pat Whitman. On the 20th, I had lunch with Gerard, who offered to recommend my essay on Wieners to the new magazine, *Little Caesar*, edited by Dennis Cooper. He also asked me to recommend his photographs to Alexander Liberman. That evening, I went to John Ashbery's publication party for *Houseboat Days*. Everyone imaginable was there. Frances Waldman asked me to write something for the *Poetry Project Newsletter*, which I did not do. Allen Ginsberg told me he had found *Kulchur Queen* very competent. He asked me if I needed any new poets, and I told him I did not. On the 21st, Gantt came over with the blueprint of *Turn Again To Me.* On Oct. 4th, Meredith Monk, who was scheduled to play at our annual big party, came by to check out the space. A few days later, our new Hunt Slonem painting was installed. On the 24th, the publication party for *Turn Again To Me*, by Helen Adam, took place at the Gotham.

The mysterious collages on the cover and throughout the book, in *Turn Again To Me*, are by Helen herself and are almost as good as Austè's drawings for *Stone Cold Gothic*; although Helen is not a professional visual artist. Of all the books I have published, this is one of my very favorites. Though Helen writes, for the most part, in the tradition of the old Scottish ballad, with rhyme and fixed meter, she is recognized by most avant garde poets as one of our greatest. Her themes are love, death, passion, retribution and, most of all, the supernatural, evoked with stunning power. Her mastery of the ballad form is rivalled only by Coleridge. "In And Out Of The Horn-Beam Maze" is about four children playing "in the ruined gardens of yesterday." One by one, they each run into a haunted maze at the garden's end. I remember Helen expressing great interest in the maze-like Serra sculpture on the grounds of our country house. I doubt that it ever had any supernatural associations for Serra, but I myself have always felt a spooky sensation walking through it. In Helen's poem, only Flora found the center of the maze and so disappeared forever. In "The Fair Young Wife," on old man near the end of life takes to himself a fair young wife, and gets what he deserves. She turns into a werewolf and devours him. In "Ballad of The Boding Well," another man gets what he deserves. Galdarvin, the harper, is a great man with the ladies, but he tires of love and women and decides to go to sea. In a last gesture of arrogance, he throws his ring into the Boding Well, where the great witch, in the form of a spider, lives. He hears the cry "woe" as it sinks. As he is congratulating himself on being rid of love and women, the sorceress draws him back to shore, where she devours him. In "The Queen O'Crow Castle," Callastan, who walks with an angel and scorns women, falls in love with the queen. He breaks down the door of her chamber, where she is guarded by a devil; and, the next morning, nothing is left of him but a fire blasted bone. On the other hand, in "Apartment At Twin Peaks," Helen turns her malignant humor on an extravagant housewife. In "Sphynx Celebration," the goddess turns her back on the pretentious and phony, and chooses the true poets for her own.

On the 25th of October, I had lunch with John Myers, still loyal to him. He had liver damage, due to his alcholism, and was on the wagon. That evening, we went to a party at Larry Rivers'. All of the New York School was there, both first and second generations. On the 28th, we discussed the projected Ellsworth Kelly sculpture with Leo Castelli. On Nov. 3rd, Charles North came over to discuss his book. From the 5th to the 14th of the month, we were in Beverly Hills, and on the 7th, Dennis Cooper came over to meet me. He was shy and awkward, didn't swim and was allergic to the sun. He left before lunch. On the 8th, David Antin came up; and we talked for two and half hours. Back in New York, our annual big party took place on the 17th; it was one of our best. Allen came with Vosnyesenski and showed him my books. Tom Armstrong, the director of the Whitney, was there. Meredith played and sang magnificently; and, since it was Morty's birthday, she gave us a signed score. Larry Rivers and I discussed the next evening of artists who write, and everyone admired me in my new Chloe gown and gold collar by Robert Lee Morris. Allen said I looked like the Queen of the Nile. On the 22nd, I had lunch with Rochelle, who was discouraged about the theatre and was deeply into poetry. On the 25th, Gantt and Charles North came over to discuss type faces. Charles was very precious and wanted 11 on 13 type instead of standard 10 on 12. For the copyright page, which is obviously important, he wanted type so small you could hardly see it and cream colored paper instead of white. The next day, I went to Soho and, once again, discussed the Kelly sculpture with Castelli.

On Dec. 2nd, we went to one of Alex Katz's great parties. There, I spoke to Tom Armstrong, Kenneth Koch, Michael Brownstein, Red Grooms, Stephen Antonakos, John Button and Irv Sandler. On the 7th, Ellsworth came to the country to pick a site for his sculpture, which is a magnificent stainless steel column, twenty-six feet high. It reflects the grass and trees and sways in the wind. A few days later, we had dinner at the Pousette Dart's. We had a lot of trouble finding the place, until Richard came out and led us in. On the way out, we got stuck in a snow drift and had to be towed away. On the 15th, I had lunch with Anne. She was very interested in what I told her about my life and thought I should write a full scale autobiography. On the 20th, I had lunch with John Myers, who was drinking again and seemed old and tired. On the 28th, I went to the 90th birthday party of Frances Steloff of the Gotham Book Mart; and finally, on the 31st, we gave a New Year's Eve party for our neighbors in the country.

CHAPTER VI

1978-1981

For most of the month of January, 1978, we were in Europe. When we returned, I worked on Lewis Warsh's proofs; and, on the 30th, Anne brought me Mary Ferrari's manuscript. On the 31st, I started taking notes on David Antin's works, and continued for much of February. On the 15th of the month, I had lunch with John Giorno, at La Caravelle, who was back from seven months in Nepal, and started writing on David. On the 17th, I gave a dinner party for the Katzes, the Schwartzes and the Solomons; and, a couple of days later, the Pousette Darts came for lunch. On the 25th, at Holly's gallery, Morty refused to buy an organdy Kim McConnell, because he said it looked like one of his $1.98 numbers. It was only $800.00; and, a few years later, we were to pay $10,000.00 for a McConnell. At the end of the month, Mary came over and talked and talked; and, at the beginning of March, I gave a dinner party for Lotte Lenye, Margo and the Economous. From the 11th to the 20th, we were in California; and, on the 28th, I had lunch with Gerard, who had sent some photographs of Wieners and an interview with him to Dennis Cooper to accompany my essay.

On April 1st, I bought both a Pousette Dart drawing and a Youngerman drawing. On the 3rd, the first poetry reading of the season took place at the MOMA. Maureen Owen introduced Steve Hamilton, Yuki Hartman and Harry Mathews. Yuki's rendition of his famous poem about a Chinese restaurant was marvelous. The next day I went to a meeting of the Friends of the Poetry Project, chaired by Ron Padgett. Present were Ted Greenwald, the art dealer Donald Droll, Bob Cummings, curator of drawings at the Whitney, and the lawyer, Carl Lobell. On the 10th, the second poetry reading of the season took place. Ted Berrigan introduced John Godfrey, Alice Notley and Jim Brodey. Godfrey was weak; Notley was great; Brodey was sensational. The next day I had lunch with John Myers, who seemed to have everything under control. On the 16th, Lotte Lenye brought Allan J. Lerner over, who came with his seventh wife, and appeared to be a charming and cultured man. The next day, the third poetry reading of the season took place, artists who write. Jennifer introduced Michelle Stuart, Richard Pousette Dart and Carl Andre. Stuart was poor, Pousette Dart read too long and only stopped when Morty started clapping; but Andre was terrific. A few days later, the Whitney picked up the John Duff sculpture we had given them. On the 22nd, we went to a cocktail party at Paula's in honor of Grovesnor; and, on the 24th, the publication party for Lewis Warsh's *Blue Heaven* took place at the Gotham. At the party, Charles North drove me and Gantt crazy with questions about his book. The next day we went to a party at the studio of painter, Natvar Bhavsar, which was a brawl.

Blue Heaven has a cover by George Schneeman, a favorite of the poets. In this book, bland and accurate descriptions of everyday life pass smoothly into imaginative leaps. The tone is always cool. In "Cambridge General," we are told it is too cold to picnic and so the poet is eating at home. A matter of fact description of sunlight and clouds passes into the highly metaphorical "rays of gray flowers, operating like an assembly line to chisel the October air." Ducks and swans on the lake pass into "gauze beaks like home fries." The tone never changes; the surface never breaks. Nurses in sweaters, autumn leaves, the color of grape juice, and a goldfish bowl filled with clear water give way to "the gold is in the flowers" and "the magnet inside the brown pot holder is given." In "Chestnut Mare," realistic descriptions of a snow capped mountain peak, footprints in the snow, a big plow and cars with treads skidding pass into skiers lost in thought, energy flowing into the minds of tired horses and a young girl leaping from a horse's back and running into the snow. In "Armed Escort," exact and scientific accounts of the act of breathing pass into "carrying on a conversation with a large puppet or dummy." I would suspect that Lewis would say that all these images are of the same order, since they are woven into a seamless fabric.

On May 3rd, I worked on Charles North's manuscript, *Leap Year*; and, the next day, Charles and Gantt came to go over it. The day after that, Steve Hamilton, Ted's protegé and Blake's friend from Lawrenceville, came to dinner. He brought a manuscript, but it was far too short to make a book. On the 11th, I had lunch with John Giorno at Lutece and gossiped of this and that; and, on the 12th, I went to my 30th Barnard reunion. A couple of days later, Larry Rivers came for lunch in the country to pick a site for his sculpture. He brought his three daughters along without letting us know in advance. Miraculously, we had enough food. On the 18th, Stuart Lavin came over to discuss plans for his book; and, a few days later, we visited John Myers and Arthur Cady in their new house in Brewster. On the way home, we stopped at the factory to pick a site for the Stromeyer sculpture. We already had a Milkowski, a Buckman and a 56 foot Liberman there. On the 24th, I went to John Giorno's cocktail party for his Buddhist guru H. H. Dudjom Rimpoche in his residence at 19 West 16th Street and, later, to a big benefit reading at the church. A few days later, the Schwartzes came to the country for the weekend with Michael; and Lenye came to dinner.

On June 3rd, John Myers and Arthur Cady came to the country for the weekend. John was subdued. On the 6th, I was photographed and interviewed by *Avenue* magzine; and, the next day, we went to the Party In The Garden at the MOMA. Later in the month, the Violis came for lunch; and Paul and I discussed the next season's poetry readings. From the 28th of June to the 21st of July we were in Europe. On Aug. 7th, Gantt came over with Charles' final proofs; and Charles and his wife, Paula, also came over with Paula's cover, hand lettered title page and other drawings. They made a great fuss about the exact placement of this material. On the same day, my essay on Wieners came out in *Little Caesar*.

On Aug. 13th, Morty and I flew to Denver to attend classes at the Jack Kerouac School of Disembodied Poetics at the Naropa Institute in Boulder. We went there at the invitation of Anne Waldman in order for me to write an article about the school. On the 14th, I walked into Tom Veitch's class late. This was unavoidable, because it was impossible for me to extract any information from any of the poets involved as to who was teaching at what hours. I finally called the registrar's office at the Naropa Institute the day before I left New York. They gave me this information, but failed to tell me that the poetry classes were not held at the Naropa Institute itself but at the Casey Junior High School several blocks away. When I arrived, Tom was reading from the "Secret Inscription In The Great Magic Papyrus Of Paris" (Greek, 1st century A.D. or earlier). This was part of an anthology of spiritual poetry, which Tom had edited as a text for his course. He then read from Liu Hua-Yang, a Taoist poet (date unknown) a poem called "From Hui Ming Ching." He encouraged the poets to try to draw comparisons between the two poems. He said the first author was overwhelmed by powerful forces. Discussion by the students followed concerning where the author stood in relation to the poem. Tom said that such poems may reveal either the greatness of the self or the emptiness of the self, and added that such poets, or possibly even Whitman, may have been "realized beings." Tom then asked the class what was the significance of light and radiance. Though it was generally agreed that these were properties of the non-phenomenal world, I asked if light and radiance did not usually symbolize God. Tom, with a faint trace of displeasure, answered yes light and radiance did usually symbolize God, but he didn't think these poets were trying to symbolize anything. They were attempting to realize real states of consciousness. He also added that the Taoists were not theists. He then said that the two poems conveyed two different perceptions of the same thing. The first poet was still involved in process; whereas the second had already passed through awakening, so that everything that had come before had never really happened.

From there, he went into a discussion of alchemy, which he said was not about the transformation of metals but about the transformation of the soul. He then discussed Shankara (India 686–718 A.D.), of whom he told us some biography. He was one of the Brahmin caste, and, at the age of ten, had knowledge of all the learned books. He grew tired of book learning, and resolved to seek for the meaning of existence. He met an old seer, who sent him to his disciple to learn Yoga. He one day met an untouchable, and, like a true Brahmin, ordered him out of the way. The untouchable shamed him by saying that if there was only one God, there couldn't be different kinds of men. He later, after having learned this lesson, established the first monastic orders in India. The first poem in Tom's text, by Shankara, "From Morning Meditation," seems like a good example of the realized state. However, Tom read from another poem of his, "From Hymn To The Goddess Who Destroys The Cities Of The Three Demons," and commented that his relationship to the divine was so erotic that he must still have been in the state of process rather than the fully realized state he claimed. Tom then read from "The Odes of Solomon" (early Christian songs, Greek, 1st century), which illustrates his view that the world of process or becoming has no real existence, that emptiness is the ultimate state. It seemed to me that both Tom and his students had more interest in primitive Christianity and Eastern religion than in any of the established Christian churches. Tom plainly said that he didn't like the spirit of the West, and saw it beginning to crumble through the onslaught of influences from the East. He touched on the Kabbalah and Jewish mysticism briefly, but didn't seem too involved. There are no passages from the Kabbalah or any other Jewish mystical writing in Tom's anthology.

The first ten minutes of Allen Ginsberg's class, on Aug. 14th, were devoted to silent meditation. He then asked his students what they had learned about the structure of the haiku. He defined it as first flash, second recognition, third afterthought. He also spoke of it as two polarized thoughts fused by a flash of recognition. He chose as his model the famous haiku of Basho about the frog jumping into the water. There have, of course, been many translations of this classic; but Allen's version was, "Old pond, Frog jump, Kerplunk." He then went on to say that the pond was the void and the jump of the frog was the world of names and forms. He said that, ideally, the haiku should contain emptiness, form and a blissful or humorous recognition of the relationship between the two. Another definition might be heaven, earth and the men that unite them both. Allen then went on to conclude that the point was the common nature of the poetic investigation of mind and the meditative investigation of mind.

Next, he discussed Kerouac's *Mexico City Blues* and read from the work in his usual impressive manner. He said that for American poetics Kerouac comes closest to the subtle recording of ordinary American mind-time. He mentioned that Kerouac wanted to be considered a jazz poet blowing choruses on Sunday. He managed to demonstrate how Kerouac succeeded in expressing *all* parts of the mind, and gave a really great rendition of his *sound*. He then quoted Whalen's statement, "My poetry is a graph of the mind moving." This, of course, he pointed out, applies to Kerouac's writing and also to the three stages of the haiku, which he said to be basic to cognition. He added that all he said applied to his own thought processes in writing poetry. Allen reaffirmed Kerouac's well known theory about the importance of spontaneous writing with no revision. He spoke of the fruitlessness of the academic poet trying too hard to say something smart. He went on to say that clear artistic and psychological truth came through many of Kerouac's superficially meaningless sounds, that he had a marvelous grasp of his own mind. Though Kerouac invented speed writing, which violated all the academic precepts of the day, his thoughts never failed to come through clearly. He firmly believed revision altered the pattern of the mind. Allen added that you cannot walk through the same river twice, and if the mind is shapely, the poem will be shapely. He also said he was surprised to hear that Duncan agreed with many of Kerouac's precepts.

Allen then went on to say that Kerouac had said: "Don't stop to think of words, think of the picture." He commented, however, that, whereas Burroughs' mind was mostly pictorial, Kerouac leaned more toward pure sound and word play, and was very much influenced both by bebop and his own Kanuck language. By way of pointing out the importance of the poet being true to his own natural speech patterns, he mentioned that Reznikoff came of Russian Jewish parentage, and quoted Reznikoff's line in which he compares tug boats to "beetles stepped on." He then spoke of Kerouac's "nonsense" as the "subsence" of the mind and of his archetypal reflections, hitherto repressed by everyone else. Whereas Williams worked with the American speech around him, he nevertheless wrote "composed" poems. Kerouac, on the other hand, was more concerned with the *quotidian sound* of the mind. Kerouac was interested in mind sounds, Williams in household sounds. Though there had been previous automatic writing, surrealist or Dada, while it was spontaneous, it was also literary. Kerouac, however, changed the "terms of the craft," just as Keats had done with the Augustan couplet. After class, I went up and told Allen that I had only recently read *Mexico City Blues*, that I had read many of Kerouac's novels through the years but had only just begun to read his poetry. I said I felt he was at his greatest in his poems, that the essence of Kerouac came through in his poetry. Allen agreed, and I decided I had to begin to read all the rest of Kerouac's poems.

In Anne Waldman's class on Aug. 15th, she shifted so rapidly from one subject to another that I found it very difficult to follow her drift.

I did, however, manage to extract three main themes: the importance of Gertrude Stein, the fact that everything is equal and everything is the same, and the importance of loss of self in order to create. Anne began her class with a discussion of Rocky Flats and the anti-nuke demonstrations there. Oddly, she compared the landscape of this place with Stein and her endeavors to bring everything in her mind into words. She said that this was because of the flatness of the landscape where everything was equal and everything was the same. She then turned to a discussion of time in art, and spoke of how Robert Wilson expanded time. She also spoke of Christopher Knowles, the autistic genius or "idiot savant," who also is involved with time in the way Stein was. She then brought up Stein's *Ida*, a late novel, stopped, and began to talk about Stein's essay "What Are Masterpieces?" She dropped the subject again to talk about how to approach phenomena, facts, how to absorb them and how to write about them. She cites, as an example of the radical adherence to fact, Andy Warhol's novel, *A*, which is entirely based on straight tape recordings. Andy's public display of his wounds, she said, was another extreme way of dealing with fact. She mentioned that when LeRoi Jones was at Boulder, he insisted that all the most hideous facts must be dealt with nakedly. She also mentioned that Allen had sometimes made use of the tape recorder.

She went on with Marshall McLuhan and his hot and cold media. She seemed to be groping toward some definition of experience, or an effort to help her students define experience and relate to phenomena. She said Burroughs writes from everything he sees and also from his dreams. She continued that Michael Brownstein did similar things in his novel, *Country Cousins*. She mentioned that Stein had said memory was not an issue in writing, although she herself was able to write pure American while living in Paris. Finally, Anne read two of her own stories from *Baby Breakdown*, and said they were influenced by Stein. The influence was quite evident. At last, she returned to the discussion of *Ida*, whom, she said, was a glamorous figure who didn't do anything except meditate on her life with dogs. Anne said this was all about how people are objects and objects are people, and everything is the same. She then read a good deal from *Ida*, and said it was an indiscriminate straightforward account of many objects. She turned to Donald Sutherland's biography of Stein and his remarks on Ida, whom, he said was a publicity saint like the heroines of romance or like the great movie stars. Stein, he said, maintains an atmosphere of legend. Anne paused to say we all live in a Steinian world, where all things are of equal importance, anything can be a subject for art, everything is no more than a state of mind.

She returned to Sutherland's comments on *Ida*, who spoke of Stein's orientalizing, of her basing Ida on the character of the Duchess of Windsor. He said that she was seeking for her essence. At last, Anne went back to "What Are Masterpieces?" She said, it was a subject involving the human mind and identity, the relationship of human nature to the human mind and the relationship of the human mind to the creative act. Knowledge is *not* what makes masterpieces, nor is identity or memory. Neither have talking or human nature anything to do with the creation of masterpieces. Rather there must be a *loss* of identity in order to create masterpieces. By way of illustration, she read a story she had written in collaboration with Bernadette Mayer while on an airplane. Anne reemphasized her point. In order to create you must lose yourself, "get lost." She concluded the session by reading some of her notes from conversations with Edwin Denby. Edwin spoke of rereading *The Autobiography of Alice B. Toklas*, and how much he loved it. He said he began to read Stein in the 20's, and she was the first to write real American. He warned, however, that one can only read her poems when all grown up. The negro dialect of Melantha, he admitted, was curious, but the rhythm was right. He maintained that it was through listening to Alice that Gerturde got everything clear and straight. He concluded that trying to find in Stein a sentence that makes sense was like trying to get an opinion out of Shakespeare.

I'm afraid my comments on Peter Orlovsky's class, on August 15th, must be very brief, because he hardly spoke at all. He devoted the whole session to having his students read their poems aloud. Peter kept looking very serious and saying "hum." I don't mean to suggest at all that Peter was playing dumb. Actually, he kept asking the students very probing questions. I gathered the direction of his probing was to discover whether or not the students' images had any real basis in their own experience and whether their emotions were phony or not. Although his questions were highly intelligent and very much to the point, he never actually followed them up with any critical comment.

Tom began his class on August 16th, by passing out copies of the Colorado Daily with information on the front page about the protestors at Rocky Flats, the site of a plutonium plant, where it was thought the neutron bomb might be built. He then passed out poems by his students, which he had read, and discussed their work with them. Since I didn't see these poems and couldn't overhear Tom's comments very clearly, I cannot comment on them. He then asked his students what they had done with their assignment, which had been to either write, find or translate a spiritual poem. One student read a poem by Irving Layton. Another read a translation he had written of Buccati. This was supposed to be about drugs, but not actually real drugs, rather about wild and funny ways to achieve ecstatic states. Another student read a poem of his own called "On The Possibility Of Love," while still another read both some of his friend's and some of his own. Finally, Tom read a poem by Allen Ginsberg from his anthology of spritual poetry. This lead me to ask a question that had been very much on my mind through most of the previous discussion. I said to Tom, I have just finished reading *The Luis Armed Story*. I have read *Eat This*; I have, in fact, read all of your published works, including the piece of yours I published myself in *Kulchur 19*. What, I asked, is the relationship of your work to all this ancient religious poetry we have been discussing? Tom replied, "Lita, that story of mine that you published, 'Yoga Exercises,' is a perfect example of a spiritual story." For those who do not possess a copy of *Kulchur 19*, I can only say that it is pure Veitch, very very funny and full of highly scatological material. Tom explained that the spritual contained *everything*, that since we are all God incarnate, everything we do is spritual even if we are playing with our shit. He then read from a poem of Whitman's by way of further explanation.

I then said I really didn't know whatever made me bother to ask such a question, in view of all that I have published, and especially in view of the fact that John Giorno is one of my very best friends. Tom replied that John Giorno was indeed a very spiritual man, but that the title of his poem, "Drinking the Blood of Every Woman's Period," disgusted even him. He then continued that *all* poetry is spiritual *except* the poetry of ego drive, narcissism and limited consciousness. There was further discussion on the nature of the spiritual by the students, which led Tom to reiterate that ultimately things have no meaning, that all is emptiness. He then read some poems by Allama Prabnu (India, 12th century), "Vacanas" (songs to Siva). He commented on the surreal nature of these poems, which I also noticed, and then asked what the maimed ape with supernatural powers represented (symbolized???). I questioned if the maimed were supposed to be godlike. Tom didn't agree. A student improved on my question by saying that God was always perfect, but the prophets of God were often afflicted. The conclusion, if any, was that the maimed ape represented the lingam. Tom added that we must turn away from conventional ideas of the good to achieve expanded consciousness, a consciousness of contradiction. He said that the poet under discussion was not trying to communicate a written truth but to put us in a state of confusion, unlike the surrealists, who were only trying to break down established conventions. He said this poet was trying to test us, to set us against him (so too were the surrealists in my opinion). Tom concluded his remarks by saying that the experience of madness might lead to expanded consciousness, an opinion with which I cannot agree, despite Laing's theories. From all I know about it, mental illness is an agonizing experience, and leads neither to creativity nor a higher state of consciousness.

Allen's class, on Aug. 16th, began once again with ten minutes of silent meditation. He said of meditation that its purpose was not to check out another universe but *purposelessly* to settle in to where you are. He then spoke of the hugeness and emptiness of the space through which we pass, and added that this gives us a sense of such spaciousness we feel the mind has no roof. Allen spent less time lecturing in this class and more time reading from works which he admired. He first read from the "Kaleva, " a Finnish epic, orally transmitted for several centuries but first written down in the nineteenth century. It concerns a confrontation between two bards, one old and wise, the other young and arrogant. When they first meet, their chariots become entangled. The young man then begins to boast of all the truths he knows. When the old seer asks him if he knows anything else besides all the foolishness he has uttered, the young man continues to lie and boast further. When the elder makes fun of him, the young man challenges him to a duel, and is refused. Then the old bard begins to sing and to bewitch the young upstart and everything around him. Begging to be released, the youth offers him one of his boats, and is refused. He then offers him one of his horses, and is refused again, then offers silver and gold and is also refused. Finally, he offers his lands and is still refused. But when the young man offers his sister, the old bard is pleased, and revokes his charm.

RECENT ACQUISITIONS

Copyright
By General Idea

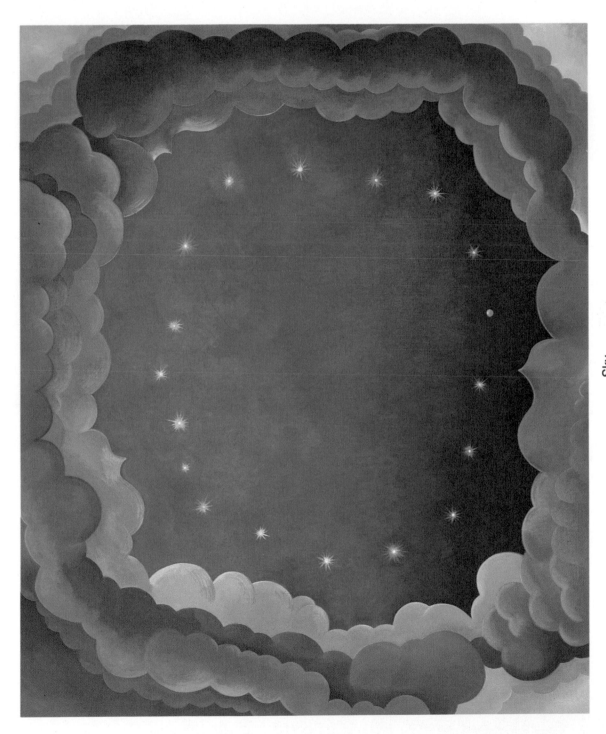

Sky
By Milan Kunc

Prudential
By Mark Kostabi

Come And Look
By Cary Smith

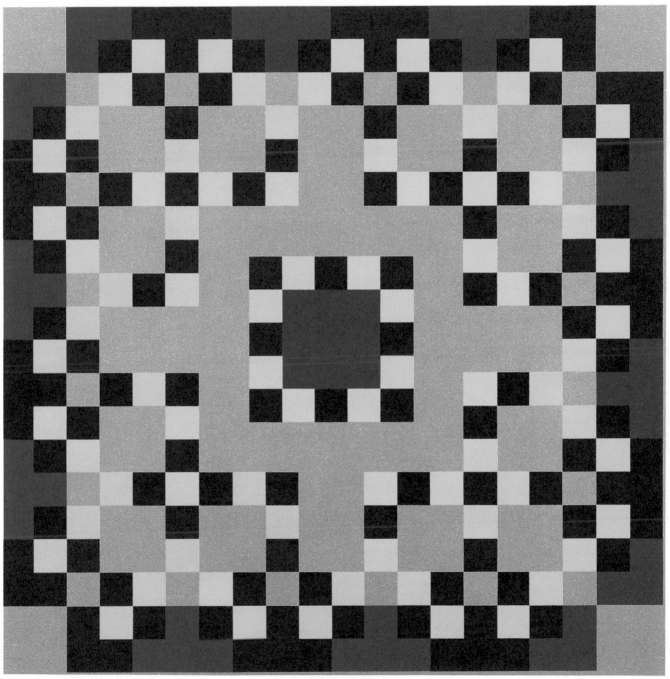

Pozion
By Gilbert Hsaio
Photo By James Dee

Light Passing
By April Gornik

Can You Remember
By Cary Smith

Fortune
By Serge Kliaving

Yes Hans, "YOU ARE REALLY QUIET"
By Austé
Photo By Jerry L. Thompson

Perfect Vehickle
By Allen McCollom
Photo BY Jerry L. Thompson

Allen read briefly again from *Mexico City Blues*, and then turned to Hart Crane, whom he called another witness to everything American, one who was trying to find a bridge between the old America and the new. He read the section from "The Bridge" about the hoboes, and then read a section which he describes as "pure breath." He read this passage with such emotion that everyone applauded spontaneously afterward. He admitted, however, that, unlike Kerouac, Crane did much revision. Allen then turned to Burroughs' *Exterminator*, and read the passage about the old colonel's reminiscences, his efforts to first bring himself back to the present and then to create D.E. (do easy). This was all, of course, very funny and, as Allen said, "home made American." He concluded his reading from Burroughs with a long comic dissertation on D.E. The class ended with a question and answer period, in which several students raised objections to Allen's precepts of spontaneous writing with no revision. He was in no way deterred from his convictions. In reply to one student, who asked what one should do when one came up against a line that wouldn't work, he said, "I guess you should just begin a new poem."

Like Allen in his second class, Anne, in her second class on Aug. 17th, devoted less time to lecturing and more time to reading from works she admired. The emphasis was very definitely on Stein. She began by playing a record of Stein reading from her own works, which was very beautiful. She then read from Stein's lectures and from *Four Saints in Three Acts*. She told us this opera, in collaboration with Virgil Thompson, was first published in 1929 in *Transition* and later in 1932. Stein first met Thompson in the winter of 1925-6, when he was at Harvard. He claimed that when he read *Tender Buttons* it changed his life. Anne explained that there is no conventional dramatic action in the work, that it is all carried through the language, which is in a conversational style. There is neither rhetoric nor conflict. The saints are supposed to be in heaven. She again compared Stein to Wilson in her use of the stage. Her stage directions are only to be imagined; they are not real props. There is no narrative. Everyone is supposed to be in a state of beatitude, and Stein's idea of the celestial life was harmony. The saints exist and converse, but don't do anything. Anne then said that Stein in her word portraits tried to tell what they were without telling stories, in her plays she tried to tell what happened without telling stories. She spoke of her influence on such people as Clark Coolidge, Bernadette Mayer, Lew Welch, Jackson MacLow,

111

Meredith Monk and David Antin, and read three of Coolidge's poems. She said Stein had had a great influence on poet's theatre but not on conventional theatre. When a student asked about her influence on John Giorno, Anne replied that she thought it was only in the use of repetition. I agreed with her in almost all respects, except the influence on Antin, who is so *intellectual*, so full of *meaning* and so intent on getting that meaning across. Anne replied that, in his case, she thought the influence lay in his emphasis on the oral.

On Aug. 17th, after Anne's class, we flew home to New York. On the 21st, I started my essay on the Kerouac school; and, a few days later, my new wallsize book case was installed in my newly decorated office, once Louis' room. The cabinet for my papers was installed on the 28th, which enabled me to rescue them from drawers and closets throughout the apartment and to frame and hang Joe's drawings from *Bean Spasms* and *Album*. Also on the 28th, Charles and Paula came to check the drawings in the blueprint of *Leap Year*, and spent two hours going over the whole book again. On Sept. 1st, I received a letter from Dennis Cooper asking to see my essay on the Kerouac school. On the same day, *Avenue* magazine came out with a two page writeup on me, written by Ally, and accompanied by a full page photograph. I was thrilled. On the 3rd, Lenye came for lunch and looked great. I thought it was amazing for a woman who had just had two cancer operations. Later in the month, I had lunch with John Myers, who looked and sounded OK; and, a couple of days later, I met with Paul, Gerritt, Pat and Barbara Pine to discuss the next season's poetry readings. On the 20th, we met with Leo and Ellsworth at Lipincott, the sculpture fabricator, to view Ellsworth's magnificent piece. Afterwards, we all went for dinner at the Cremaillere to celebrate.

On Oct. 1st, Ellsworth came down to our country house to place a marker for the installation of his sculpture, and stayed for lunch. Lenye came over later and picked up a copy of *The Intricate Image*. Later on, in the city, I bought a Christopher Knowles from Holly. It contains four canvasses, two large and two small, each representing clocks saying 8:30. I assumed it symbolized time; I don't know what happened at 8:30. On the 13th, we had dinner at the Economous, who are among my oldest and best friends. Rochelle was her usual ebullient and crazy self, George solid and straight as always. On the 20th, I was furious because Gantt, who was getting senile, was late with *Leap Year*. He delivered only the paper backs to Gotham and no books to me. I had to send the nervous nut Charles over to Gotham to see his book. He was my most troublesome author since Kenneth Koch and Bill Berkson, who, like Kenneth, kept rewriting. That evening I had a meeting of the Friends of the Poetry Project at my apartment; and, on the 23rd, the publication party for *Leap Year* took place at the Gotham.

Although I have complained of Charles' pestiness during its production, I certainly do not mean to condemn his book. It has a lovely wraparound cover and drawings by his wife, Paula. Although the metaphors leap, such as "every word rings like the ear of a spaniel," the tone is gentle; and there is much nature imagery. One can detect the influence of James Schuyler, as well as Tony Towle. "Japanese Woman Beside The Water" is a good example of his style, where raining outdoors is compared to warmed frozen pizza. In the title poem, "Leap Year," the "roof is clearly melting into the sky," and "the way out" is to "paint everything turquoise." Nature's "green" is a recurrent motif, as is evident in the lovely poem "Mackerel Sky." In "The Poem And The Novel For Francis Lefevre," "the poem is brilliant orange, owing money to everyone," and "the novel sinks in misted skies." In "The Smart & Final Iris Co.," there is much lush imagery; a window with some hyacinths, straggling roses, black eyed susans and irises for hair. The poems escape being pretty through Charles' strong intellectual control and the breadth of his metaphors.

On Oct. 25, I had lunch with John Giorno at Lutece, who asked me to lend him $1,500.00 with his Warhols as collateral. After speaking to Morty, I told him we would buy his "Vote McGovern" poster (with the evil face of Nixon on it) for that price. John was pleased with this arrangement. He needed the money for his latest LP record project. On the 28th, we went to a benefit, at CBGB's for St. Mark's, which had recently had a fire. There was a poetry reading there accompanied by a punk rock band, which I loved. I smoked so much of the pot that was offered to me (I never had any of my own), and got so drunk, that Morty and Ted Berrigan had to assist me to a cab. It was one of the best times of my life. On the 31st, I had lunch with Gerard, who looked handsome in a vested suit, a contrast to the weird garb he used to wear in the 60's. We made small talk; and he gave me Stuart Lavin's manuscript *Let Myself Shine*, which I looked over on Nov. 1st. On the 7th, I had lunch with Rochelle. As was usual at our lunches, we made small talk rather than serious literary discussion.

A few days later, Larry Rivers called to invite me to his golden oldies show, reworkings of famous paintings from the 50's and 60's. He also inquired about his invitation to my party; since he had just gotten back from Europe, and hadn't gotten it through the mail. On the 14th, I had lunch with Anne and Frances and asked Anne for pictures of the Kerouac School, which Dennis wanted to accompany my essay; and on the 16th, my annual big party took place. The next day, Gantt, Paul Violi and Charles North came to go over my essay on David Antin. It was too long for magazine publication, and so Paul and Charles had agreed to publish it as a Swollen Magpie Press pamphlet. A couple of days later, we went to Larry's studio to discuss his suggestions for a sculpture. Everything he showed us was too erotic to put outdoors, especially in the same county as Morty's factory. Finally, we settled on "The Swimmers," a shallow painted relief in canvas and plastic, which we later translated into painted aluminum and plastic. Unlike our Katz painted cutouts, it has stood up well through the years. Between the 26th of November and the 6th of December, we were in California; and, soon after our return, went to dinner at the Schwartzes', where I spent most of the time talking to John Ashbery and his friend, David Kermani. On the 19th, I went to a meeting of the Friends of the Poetry Project at Morris Golde's, and, on the 29th, David Antin and I were photographed for the cover of my Swollen Magpie Press pamphlet. On the day before New Year's Eve, we went to Frances' eggnog party; and, on New Year's Eve, we went to a party in painter Hunt Slonem's loft.

On Jan. 2nd, 1979, we flew to London and from there to Cairo. The pyramids and sphinx dwarfed all jaded expectations in their massive grandeur. Also in Cairo, we visited a 10th century synagogue, a 7th century Coptic church and a 14th century mosque. Next we took a day trip to Suez, which was a bore. On the other hand, our trip to Memphis, where we saw the great statue of Rameses and the alabaster sphinx, was very exciting. From there, we went to Sukhara and walked through the sands of the Sahara to see the step pyramid, the oldest in Egypt. It had just recently been opened, and there was still color on the walls. Finally, we took Ethiopian air lines from Cairo to Frankfurt, which Morty called "the airline with a spear." Actually, it was an American plane with an American pilot and ordinary airline food. The only thing exotic about it was the beautiful Ethiopian stewardesses with their long robes. On the 19th, we flew home from Paris; and, the

114

next day, *The Little Magazine In America* came out, with my essay on *Kulchur* magazine. On the 23rd, I saw Stella's Indian Birds at Castelli, which almost levitated me off the ground. There I met Irv Sandler, who very flatteringly, introduced me to his students as a great publisher of poetry. The next day, George Plimpton gave a cocktail party for all the little magazine editors, at which, very arrogantly, he never showed up himself. Toward the end of the month, I interviewed Helen Adam in preparation for writing about her; and, on the 31st, Holly and Horace came up to the country to install the Knowles and look at the Kelly.

The first half of February was taken up by my work on Stuart Lavin's book and my David Antin pamphlet, and also, in taking notes on Helen's poems, which I loved doing. On the 11th, we went to Horace's 50th birthday party, where, naturally, most of the art world was present; and, a few days later, Janine Pommy Vega came over to discuss her book, *The Bard Owl*. In the second half of the month, I wrote my essay on Helen, for which the words gushed forth; and on the 23rd I gave a dinner party for Arthur and Carol Goldberg, recent collectors at that time, and the Economous. On the first day of March, we went out to dinner with John Myers and Arthur Cady, which was an uninspiring evening. The next day, senile Gantt forgot our appointment to go over *Let Myself Shine*, Stuart's book; and, after we returned from a ten day trip to Calofirnia, he finally came over with the blueprint of that book and the final page proofs of *David Antin/Debunker of the "Real."*

On April 2nd, the first poetry reading of the season took place at the MOMA. Armand Schwerner introduced David Antin, Anselm Hollo and Clark Coolidge. I gave the general introduction to the reading and introduced Armand. Antin was *great*, Hollo very good and Coolidge, in my opinion at least, very boring. On the 9th, the second poetry reading of the season took place. Joe Ceravalo introduced Mary Ferrari, Bob Holman and Philip Lopate. I introduced Joe, and made the mistake of calling his book, *Fits of Dawn, Tits of Dawn*. When he got up to speak, he said, "I loved that *Tits of Dawn*. It was originally called *Fits of Dawn*; but if it is ever reprinted, I am going to change it to *Tits of Dawn*. Everyone collapsed in laughter, including me. Mary was moving, Philip very witty, Bob totally hilarious. He came up with a paper bag over his head; whereupon the audience shouted "Tear It Off!," which he did. *Tear To Open* was the title of the book he passed around. He sang most of his poems and was simply terrific.

115

On the 16th, the third poetry reading of the season took place. Alice Notley introduced Ron Padgett, Kenneth Koch and Kate Farrell. Kenneth and Ron were in good form; but Kate, Kenneth's girl friend at the time, was poor. Later in the month, Lenye came to lunch and was as marvelous as ever. She had made another of her remarkable recoveries, this time from a broken elbow and shoulder. The next day, I had lunch with John Giorno at La Caravelle, and agreed to write a piece on Giorno Poetry Systems records. On the 25th, we went to Ellsworth's opening at the Metropolitan and then to a supper party given by his dealers, Castelli and Blum Helman. On the 27th, we went to dinner at the Schwartzes'; and, on the 30th, the publication party for *Let Myself Shine* and *David Antin/Debunker of the Real*," took place at the Gotham.

Stuart Lavin, at the time of the publication of *Let Myself Shine*, was, except for his Four Zoas Press, almost totally unknown to the New York poetry world. I had been urged to publish him by my very good friend Gerard Malanga. I thought Kulchur was strong enough to bring out such an unknown, and I thought his book was good. Nevertheless, not a single copy was sold at his publication party, and Andreas Brown returned them all the next day. Later on, the book began to have a respectable sale. Though completely isolated, Lavin has succeeded in writing poems which meet the criteria of avant garde literature. "Journey To A Lone Star," is almost pure statement, but the politics are right. "What Poems Are About" looks like a simple statement, but the transitions are non-linear. "Command Performance," both traditional and contemporary, deals with the relationship between love and art. "All My Loves Are One Love" takes a rather pretentious view of the role of the poet; Lavin is not cool. Despite the fact that he does not meet the standards of the super cool New York School, Lavin's poems are not without substance and value; and I have always felt that this exercise in courage on my part was good for Kulchur.

On May 2nd, I did an exhausting line count on Ted Greenwald's manuscript, *Licorice Chronicles*. This is one long poem composed of words that, for the most part, don't make any sense. It is not one of my favorite books; but, like Clark Coolidge, Greenwald represented an important trend of the time, related to minimal art. The next day, I interviewed Joe Brainard, who stayed for dinner; and, a couple of days later, we approved the macquette for Larry's sculpture. On the

11th, we had dinner with the Solomons; and, a few days later, we went to the opening of Andy Warhol's fruit serigraphs. Andy asked me if I wanted him to sign my jewelry. I was wearing some striking gold jewelry by Robert Lee Morris with earrings by Man Ray; and, at that time, it was common for an artist to appropriate any object that struck his fancy and claim it as a work of art. Later in the month, Leo Castelli came to the country to see the Kelly and stayed for lunch. A couple of days later, the Eshlemans came over for conversation and a drink. Finally, at the end of the month, Ron, Pat and Wayne Padgett came up to the country, with Alice Notley and her two sons, Anselm and Edmund.

It was in May, 1979, that I attempted to commit suicide, having reached the end of my rope through prolonged and unsuccessful fasting. Although I had always previously been slim and had a good figure, my menopause disturbed my metabolism. I went on the Optifast diet, now popular, then in the experimental phase. It involved dissolving a diet supplement powder in water four times a day and neither eating nor drinking anything else. It supplied 450 calories a day. In twenty-three days, I lost eighteen pounds. I then attempted to maintain this weight loss by fasting three or four days a week. As soon as I stopped fasting, I gained all of the weight back. Complaining about it one night, Morty said in a cutting voice, "Sure, you fast all week and then eat and drink like a pig." Taking a box of sleeping pills out of the medicine cabinet, I swallowed them. Morty and Louis took me to Lenox Hill Hospital where they pumped my stomach out. They wanted to send me up to Harlem Hospital for psychiatric testing, but Morty fought for me and succeeded in obtaining my release. Frightened at what I had done, I went back into psychotherapy with a new psychiatrist, Dr. M. Dorothea Kerr. After a while, I gave up the doctor who had prescribed the Optifast diet and just let myself get fat.

During most of August, I was engaged in taking notes on Joe, in preparation for writing first on his books and then on his art. It was my first attempt at writing on art. On Aug. 2nd., Gerard brought over the Brainard color transparencies and black and white contacts. On the 4th, Lenye and Billie Harkavy came to dinner. They were both amazing ladies in their eighties, who had smoked and drank since their early teenage years and had enjoyed every minute of it. On the 12th, the Violis and the Norths came to lunch; and we discussed the

next season's poetry readings. On the 7th of September, the now se-
nile Gantt brought Ted Greenwald's corrected page proofs a week late.
The next day we went to Brad's opening, followed by a party at Holly's
which was tout New York. In the middle of the month, I had lunch
with Gerard, and, a few days later, went to Jack Youngerman's studio
to look at his sculpture. From there, I went to Morty's office to meet
with Sylvia Stone, Al Held's wife at that time, and see slides of her
sculpture. We spoke of Al's long time refusal to come to my apart-
ment until I moved his painting out of the foyer, lest it be damaged
at one of my parties. It was too big to put anywhere else. Sylvia said
it was ridiculous, but that Al would not be the first one to give in. Fi-
nally, on the 28th, my grandson, Louis Hornick III was born, nicknamed
Tripp for triple; and, on the 30th, the party in honor of the Kelly sculp-
ture took place in the country. Ellsworth was very charming, and I
was interested to hear that he admired Joe Brainard.

On Oct. 5th, we had dinner at the Economous, the only poets we
socialized with on this basis. The poet Bill Zavatsky, and his wife, were
also there; and we had a wonderful time. Rochelle and I signed our
books for each other. On the 9th, I bought the first of our three Richard
Kalinas from Tibor. On the same day, Ted came over to OK the blue-
print for *Licorice Chronicles*, and told me how much he liked *David
Antin/Debunker of the "Real."* On the 23rd, I had lunch with Rochelle
and told her about our estrangement from John Myers. He had re-
fused to take Morty's hand at the MOMA, because Morty did not buy
a Rivers bust of him that he wanted to sell us. A few days later, Janine
Pommy Vega came over with her manuscript; and, a few days after
that, the publication party for *Licorice Chronicles* took place at the
Gotham. It was a huge success, and Gotham sold all the books they
had. On the 1st of November, Maureen Owen came over to discuss
her forthcoming book, *Hearts In Space*; and, the next day, we had
lunch with the Eshlemans. Clayton is very nice but a little bit of a stuffed
shirt. On the 15th, our annual big party took place. The Stimulators,
a terrific punk rock band, played. Harley, the twelve year old drummer,
was fantastic. They cavorted wildly all around the living room, and
the sound was deafening. I never left the living room when they were
playing. The next day, Gantt came to go over Janine's manuscript with
me; and it was evident he was not all there anymore.

On Dec. 6th, 1979, I had lunch with Maureen at La Caravelle. She came in denim overalls and said she had never been to a French restaurant before. The next day we had dinner at La Cote Basque with John Giorno and Burroughs, whom I met for the first time. He wore his proverbial grey Fedora hat and spoke in his proverbial dry voice. He was shy, charming and a perfect gentleman. On the 13th, I read Sotère's little book about his visit to us; and, a couple of days later, we bought a Marian Loveland Miller from Tibor. A few days after that, we were Morris Golde's guests at the Nutcracker and at the Russian Tea Room; and, finally, on the 28th, I interviewed Allen about Kerouac, in preparation for writing on Kerouac's poems. He gave me a lecture on Buddhism and much information about Jack, and very generously lent me much valuable material: tapes, notebooks and a textbook on Buddhism.

On June 6th, we went to the Party in the Garden at the MOMA. There I met the famous drag queen, Jackie Curtis, dressed in a conservative men's suit. When I asked her (I always think of him as female) "What sex are you now Jackie?" She lisped "Straight Male." On the 11th, I went to outrageous Rene Ricard's publication party at Books & Co. He complained because I was not wearing jewelry and an evening dress, as was my custom at my own parties. The title of the book was *Rene Ricard 1979-1980*. The publisher was DIA. Gerard was the editor, and the party was a mob scene. Andy Warhol was there and gave me a kiss; Rene, like Gerard, had been part of his scene. From the 16th of June until the 9th of July we were in Europe. On the 14th the Schwartzes came to the country for the weekend. Gene was enthralled by the Kelly. A few days later, Ted Greenwald came over to my apartment with the cover for his book, and brought the artist, Jim Starrett. Toward the end of the month, Gerard came up for lunch and photographed all the Joe Brainards, in preparation for my essay on Joe.

Most of January and February 1980 was spent working on my essay on Kerouac. From Jan. 10th to the 24th, we were in Europe. On Feb. 2nd, we went to Neil Welliver's opening and to a party in his honor, given by the Walshes, his friends and largest collectors. In the middle of February, the painting "Night Flight," by Susan Hall, was installed in my apartment. I had special feelings about this painting, and was to use it as a front cover and title of my next book. Toward the end of the month, Janine came to go over the corrected proofs of her book, *The Bard Owl*, and brought the artist, Martin Carey, who did the drawings. On March 8th, we went to the Schwartzes' for dinner; and, on the 12th, I sat for my portrait by George Schneeman. The next day, Janine came to go over the artwork and cover of her book; and Gantt did not show up. Shortly after that I had lunch with Morris Golde and told him that Rene had threatened to cancel his reading at the MOMA because the announcement had put an accent over his name, which he did not use. Toward the end of the month, I gave a dinner party for the Schwartzes, the Goldbergs and the Economous.

On the 31st of March, the first poetry reading of the season took place at the MOMA. Maureeen Owen introduced Rene Ricard, Jamie MacInis and Bill Berkson. Rene was very moving, MacInis was superb and Bill was very good. On April 3rd my piece on the Kerouac School came out in *Little Caesar*. On the 7th, the second poetry reading of the season took place. Rochelle Owens introduced Robert Kelly, Janine Pommy Vega and Diane Wakoski, they were all terrific. Kelly, once enormously fat, had lost 240 pounds! On the 14th, the third poetry reading of the season took place. Carter Ratcliff introduced John Ashbery, Ann Lauterbach and F.T. Prince. It was a total smash. I invited John to go out to dinner with us afterwards, but he insisted that I invite all the poets that had read as well. I acceeded to his wishes; but, as soon as the reading was over, he went to the bar and got so drunk that he was unable to accompany the rest of us to dinner. On the 19th, we had lunch with the Eshlemans; and, a few days later, I discovered, to my horror, that Janine's book had turned out blue! When Janine went down to the office to pick up her books, she cursed and carried on, quite naturally. At her publication party on the 29th, Martin Carey said it was "a beautiful Zen error." In spite of his generosity, I realized that, difficult and sad though it would be, I had to get rid of Gantt.

Janine Pommy Vega was the feminine voice in the beat circle. Unlike the poets of the New York School, her poems are direct and available. Her subject matter is often drawn from nature, and her tone is personal and passionate. "San Francisco Shuffle" mourns the aging of that great city and its dreams. In "Gypsy Players," the poet, who loves the wilderness, is greeted at her campfire by an alluring band of gypsies; but she can't leave hillside, forest and hoot-owl to follow them to their "bright encampments." In "Tale of the Hunter," a hunter kills a hare and is killed by a scorpion, who is killed by a centaur. All this is seen in the constellations of Orion, Scorpius and Lepus. In "Rites of the Eastern Star" she decries dogmatic verse, tepid theatre and vague sermons to invoke the great tragedians who "knew how to wring the necks of swans." "The Birds" pays homage to the great birds of prey, sacred to the Goddess, who symbolize the vast forces of nature. In "November Landscape," the glories of nature are projected through gorgeous metaphors, "feathered brooches," "jewel encrusted birds," "extravagant fans." "Where Are You?" speaks of her need for a straying lover. "Re-Entry" beautifully describes the search for the self through "the confluence of stars," tides, floods, swamps, evening calm and cracked skulls. Janine projects her own voice through all the trends and fashions of contemporary poetry.

On May 7th, the experts came from Parke-Bernet to appraise our collection. The appreciation of our paintings was staggering. No one could be merely lucky that often. From then on Morty became my partner in art collecting. The next day, Maureen came to lunch, accompanied by the artist, John Giordano, who did the drawings for her book, and the poet, Vicki Hudspith, who did the design. A couple of days later, I bought a Peter Sarrie at OK Harris; and, on the 15th, we went to the benefactor's preview of the great Picasso exhibition at the MOMA. The next day, we returned to the exhibition for the contributing member's preview. On the 19th, I corrected the proofs for my essay on Helen, sent to me by *Sun & Moon*. Several days later, Mary Ferrari came to lunch. She was pathetically nervous and insecure for such a good poet. On the 25th, Blake graduated from law school, first in his class in scholarship and second in grades. Finally, on the 28th, we went to a party given by Susan Hall. We discussed her painting, and, for a time, thought ourselves soul sisters.

On June 1st, Red Grooms and Lenye came to lunch. Red and I discussed Picasso and agreed that we liked his synthetic cubism and surrealism better than his analytical cubism. He agreed that the MOMA's "Girl Before A Mirror" was one of the best Picassos. He said he would repair his own painting, damaged at the Walker Art Center, at no charge. The next day, John Giorno came to lunch; and I interviewed him about his Dial-A-Poem records. The day after that, we went to the Party in the Garden at the MOMA, and had another look at the Picasso show; and, on the 7th, the Smithsonian Institute toured our apartment. We were in Europe from June 12th to July 7th, and, when we returned, I worked on Maureen's proofs. They were the first proofs I received from Capital City, my new printer; and, after nineteen years with Gantt, they were the first nearly perfect proofs I had ever received. On the 10th, Gantt finally appeared in Morty's office, but without Martin Carey's drawings, which he was withholding. After some time, he returned the drawings, and at last accepted our terms for final payment. For most of the rest of the month I was busy working on Maureen's proofs and taking notes on John's LP records; but, on the 24th, we went up to Lippincott to look at Larry's sculpture. Larry did not show up.

On Aug. 6th, 1980, I finished my piece on the Giorno records; and, a couple of days later, Fee Dawson came over to pick up Maureen's manuscript, as he had agreed to write a blurb for her. We reminisced. A few days afterward, my essay on Helen came out in *Sun & Moon*; and, a couple of days after that, Larry came up to the country to pick a site for his sculpture, accompanied by a beautiful model. He told us that, now that he was fifty-five, his art was his life. While the model washed her hair, Morty took him to lunch at the Dellwood Country Club, where he ate borscht and gefilte fish. On the 15th, John Giorno came to pick up his records. He said he couldn't get another book published because he was thought of as an exclusively oral poet. Yet he couldn't perform the poems, if they weren't written down. He said he wrote his poems in longhand, often with a live microphone in hand, then typed them up and rehearsed them to develop the musical qualities inherent in the words. Then he performed them to live audiences to further develop them, and recorded and released them on LP records. And then the video was made. If his poems weren't written down, he would never be able to memorize and perform them, so the written page was very important to him. He felt very disappointed by the rejection of his manuscript by every publisher. On the 21st, Fee returned with a great blurb. We reminisced some more, and he hustled me for $100.00. A few days later, the Violis and the film maker, Hans Dudelheim came to lunch. Dudelheim said he would need $60,000.00 to $70,000.00 to make a videotape of my poetry readings.

In the months of September and October, we were very active collecting art, mostly in the area of pattern and decoration, which was then at its height. On Sept. 6th, we bought a Robert Zakanytch, on the 12th, a Judy Pfaff, on the 13th, two Richard Kalinas. On October 4th, we bought a Ben Schonzeit and two Lynda Benglis wall sculptures; and, on the 11th, we bought two Joyce Kozloff's. On Sept. 20th, I interviewed Alex Katz, in preparation for my essay "Twelve Paintings in My Collection," my first full scale piece on art. I was to interview eleven of the painters; but, since Ad Reinhardt was dead, I had to depend on his writings, edited by Barbara Rose. On the 25th, the leader of the chamber music ensemble, the Baroque Trio, came to check the space in my living room prior to playing at my annual party. A couple of days later, I interviewed Jennifer Bartlett, and, on the 22nd, Tom Wesselmann. That night we had dinner with Holly and Horace and then took them to Poets & Writers' tenth anniversary party at Roseland. On the 27th, the publication party for Mureen's *Hearts In Space* took place; and on the 31st, I interviewed Red Grooms.

There is an insistent, almost breathless rhythm in *Hearts In Space* which propels the poems from start to finish. This is most evident in the last section, "Country Rush," but is also present in the other poems as well. They are direct and available, allowing the lyric voice to rush out unimpeded. In an untitled poem, white sails, orange and tan trailer, strip of blue water, yellow light and hemlock silhouette pass through exactly right breath pauses to the poet's statement that she has never suffered from the slightest tinge of penis envy. These poems are both feminine and feminist. In another untitled poem, dedicated to Emily Dickinson, a girl working in a stationary store blurts out "I'm in love" to complete strangers, the trees go from plain green to cheeks flushed and dropping everything; baby bashes through them hooting "More!", "the landscape's gone silly;" the emperor sweeps by with imperial dragon robes; Fred Astaire sings in the grand finale crescendo "O furious excesses!" The poem ends, "O bald October I knew you when you still had hair.!" Maureen uses invocations beginning with "O" very effectively. From "Country Rush," we have the wonderful untitled poem, dedicated to the Buddha, in which Maureen eats the entire landscape on the day she arrives in the country. Surely she has an original voice.

From the 2nd of November till the 12th we were in California. Shortly thereafter, Mary Ferrari came to go over her manuscript; she was a nervous wreck. The next day we went to the Serra opening at the Hudson River Museum. He had amazed me by calling and asking us to come. On the 16th, we went to a party at the poet Yuki Hartman's place; and, the next day, I interviewed Ellsworth Kelly. On the 20th, the last of my big parties took place. Although these parties were very lively, and everyone seemed to like them; I had been less than happy about them for some time. Fifty percent of the mob were always persons unknown to me, and the stupid Pinkerton guard was never able to keep them out. The crashers enraged me; and I was also annoyed at the poets who called up and told me what other poets, unknown to me, I *had* to put on the invitation list. When my anger, long suppressed as usual, finally boiled over, I stopped giving the parties. On the 25th, I had lunch with Gerard, who looked handsome and well dressed. The next day he photographed the paintings in my apartment which I planned to write about. Later that day, I had a meeting with Andy Warhol. He came to my apartment himself, an unusual thing for him to do after he was shot. We warmly renewed our old friendship, and he gave me a long interview. The next day, Alice Notley came over to discuss her book, *Waltzing Matilda*; and, in the evening, we took Gerard up to the country with us. He told us that he was going to read at St. Mark's, for the first time in six years.

On the 2nd of December, Gerard brought his color transparencies over; and, the next day, the Rivers sculpture was installed in the country. Larry did not show up; he hasn't seen the sculpture so far. On the 4th, I interviewed Jack Youngerman, who said the best thing for an artist's career was to die. The next day we had dinner at the Economous, and enjoyed ourselves as usual; and, the day after that, we bought a Robert Kushner from Holly, as well as four Brad Davis drawings. On the 7th, Tibor, his assistant, David Kermani, and Joyce Kozloff came up to the country for lunch. A couple of days later, I interviewed Kenneth Noland; and, on the 13th, we had dinner at the Schwartzes'. A couple of days after that, we had cocktails at the Lansings'; and, on the 18th, I got Frank Stella's very secret phone number from Ellsworth. When I called him, Stella said he would not like to be interviewed but that he would answer my questions if I put them in a letter. He never answered my letter. On the 23rd, I had a meeting with the videotaper Matthew Clarke, since Dudelheim's proposal had been far too expensive; and, on the 27th, I started writing "Twelve Paintings in My Collection."

On the 3rd of January, 1981, we went out to dinner at Lutece with

John Giorno and William Burroughs. We all had a very good time. William went on for years to say "Best venison I've ever had. It was perfect." On the 6th, sections of my piece on the Giorno records came out in *The World*; and, that evening, we went to Kenward's Twelfth Night Party. There was a lavish buffet and a very in crowd. From the 9th to the 25th, we were in Europe; and, shortly after our return, we went to the Whitney Biennial, where Holly's artists made a conspicuous splash. On the same day, we bought a Sandy Skogland photograph, the famous "Revenge of the Goldfish." On the 3rd of February, I worked on Mary's proofs and prepared the manuscript of *Night Flight* for the printer. The next day, I took Mary to lunch in Soho, and bought a Jennifer Bartlett drawing for her cover. That evening, we went to a party at Holly's. We continued collecting art at a great rate in the month of February, a Randy Stevens, a Patricia Tobacco Forrester and Anne Poor's painting of our country house. We also gave a dinner party for the Violis, the Norths and the Hartmans; and I picked paper samples for *Night Flight*. I had decided to publish it myself through Kulchur, since Maureen had refused to publish it as a Telephone Book. I realized, after my first annoyance, that my plans for the book were really unsuitable for a small poetry press. Self publication enabled me to have seventeen color plates, many black and white illutrations and special embossed and coated paper. It also enabled me to have full control of the layout and design.

From the 11th to the 17th of March, we were in California. When we returned home, we went to the opening of Rochelle's play "Chuckie's Hunch," her best since "Futz." It is about an unsuccessful abstract expressionist painter who is cracking up, probably based on the character of Owens, her first husband. At the end of the month, we bought another Kushner. On the 1st of April we went to a party at Susan Hall's loft, and, on the 2nd, gave a dinner party for the Lansings, the Solomons, Kenward and his friend and accompanist Ken Dyffuk. The next day Kenward sent me a signed book and flowers; and, the day after that, we bought a Miriam Schapiro. On the 6th, the first poetry reading of the season took place at the MOMA. Bob Holman introduced Kenward Elmslie, Andrei Codrescu and Paul Violi. Kenward's high camp singing brought down the house, Andrei was good enough to follow Kenward, and Paul had a hard act to follow. On the 10th, we went to the Swids' dinner party to honor Ellsworth, which was a heavy art world scene. The next day we had lunch with the Eshlemans; and, on the 13th, the second poetry reading of the season took place. I myself, for the first time, introduced Allen Ginsberg, William Burroughs and John Giorno, all videotaped by Matthew Clarke. It was a truly marvelous reading. Besides reading a few poems, Allen sang a terrific song, which had, unfortunately, to be removed from the videotape because his accompanist refused to sign a release. William's savage indignation and acid humor came over triumphantly; and John intoned and chanted, living up to his reputation as the foremost oral poet. On the 27th, Mary's publication party for *The Isle of the Little God* took place at the Gotham. A reporter, from the *New York Times* came to the party to interview Mary and me; and, on the 29th, the writeup appeared in the Times.

The Isle of the Little God is an interesting combination of contemporary verse and Catholic imagery. Mary dedicated the poem "The Departure of Florimell" to me, an unusual thing to do. The poems are a clear and direct account of her thoughts and associations. In "Wednesday, October 14th," she is on the train to Columbia, going to study the romantic poets, while Trinidadian Sylvia takes care of her children. She thinks of her husband in Africa, who sends her children too many post cards of lions and tigers. She remembers a rather unpleasant trip to Morocco. A few hours later, her reaction is that her romantic course is terrible, because all the professor does is compare editions. In the evening she goes to a lecture on "King Lear" and compares the interpretations of the Christian Moralists and the Existentialists. She agrees with neither. In "Fiery Easter," she is the "divine flame thrower, throwing flames as far as Rome." Her flames are "beds for the saints." The Pope leaps on a flame, and she assures him that no priest will every marry her. Saint Cecilia sits on the edge of a flame and plays a harp. Her flames are "human anger and divine beauty." Saint Paul despises her. She assures Santa Maria in Trastevere that flames can be used as prayer rugs. She is on fire from head to foot and so belongs to Abelard rather than the saints. The flames are "Easter lilies turning into huge marigolds." St. Christopher leaps over the Tiber, St. Anne wears a red pants suit, St. Joseph applauds the whole idea. She sends the saints back to their tombs and thinks of "the movement of myths and realities" and the fire of Christ.

On May 1st, Alice Notley came over with her manuscript, *Waltzing*

Matilda. I worked on it until the 8th, when I did my second proof reading for *Night Flight*. A few days later, I prepared the pictorial matter of *Night Flight* for the printer. Mary Ferrari treated me to lunch on June 2nd, an unusual experience for me. The next day, I went to see the video-tape of the Ginsberg-Burroughs-Giorno reading and OK'd it. The day after that, Joe Ceravolo came over to talk about his book. From the 14th of June to July 8th, we were in Europe; and, when I returned, I corrected the page proofs for *Night Flight* and proof read *Waltzing Matilda*. On the 17th, Alice came over to pick up her proofs and give me George Schneeman's cover drawings. A couple of days later, the Violis came to lunch; and, on the 23rd, I inspected the pictorial proofs for *Night Flight*, five of which required corrections. That weekend, we went up to stay with the Economous in their house in Wellfleet. We had a wonderful time, with wonderful food and wonderful talk. At the end of the month, I had lunch with Carol Bergé; and Ted Berrigan, who had brought over Alice's proofs, agreed to do a blurb for *Night Flight*.

In August, Morty made Louis president of Louis Hornick & Co. (named after the founder, Morty's father). Louis was soon to show himself a brilliant entrepreneur and build the company up to a much larger size. On the 13th of the month, I took Mary to lunch; and she told me that Frances Waldman was very ill. A few days later, Ellsworth came to lunch in the country and stayed till 5:30; and, a few days after that, we had lunch at the Violis and discussed the next season's poetry readings. On the 11th of September, we went to a party at Holly's; and, the next day, after exerting much pressure on Morty, I bought Richard Bosman's "The Norseman," a terrifying painting based on the Norse myth "Eaters of the Dead." Shortly after that, I received Ted's marvelous blurb for *Night Flight*, which I shall never forget. On the 15th, I visited Ted and Alice and had a wonderful time. Ted went with me to the opening of Andy Warhol's great Myths show at Ronald Feldman, where I put a reserve on a painting and a print. On the 18th, I had tea at Anne's and did the cover layout of *Night Flight*; and, the next day, upon returning to the Feldman gallery with Morty, let him persuade me to buy Andy Warhol's painting "The Star" (Garbo as Mata Hari) instead of "Mammy," which I had previously selected. On the 25th, YPO toured my apartment in three shifts, one at 10am, the second at 11 and the third at noon. Afterwards we went to Estee

Lauder's mansion for a two hour tour. We expected lunch, but they served only champagne and canapés. The next day, we bought a magnificent large Neil Welliver. In the evening we went to a formal dinner at the Metropolitan Club, given by YPO and the Lauders.

On the 15th of October, we gave a vernissage for Anne Poor's painting of our country house. The next day, I had lunch with Anne Waldman and took her to the office to see the paintings there. The day after that, I visited Frances in the hospital and then had dinner at the Pousette Darts. There I met Al Freeman, Jr., who had played the lead in LeRoi's play, "The Slave," and was now acting in soaps. On the 18th, Holly, Horace and Ned Smythe came to lunch to discuss a projected sculpture of Ned's, which we never got around to commissioning; and, a few days later, I gave a dinner party for the Solomons, the Economous and the Violis. Finally, near the end of the month, I visited John Giorno at 222 Bowery, and gave him both his and Burroughs' videotapes; and, on the 31st, the Lansings came to lunch in the country. Alice's publication party took place a little before that; and, at the party, Rene cursed me and spat at me for not giving any more of my big annual parties. He was soon to get over that and become a good friend once more.

Waltzing Matilda is a collection of poems, dialogues and plays. It was an exceptionally good seller, probably because of Peter Schjeldahl's review in the Times. "Winters of Few Poems" is one of Alice's short, lyrical poems, of which I am very fond. The untitled poem beginning "She gets older" is a marvelous example of these moving personal poems. These continue until page 36, where the first of her plays, "Nights In The Gardens Of Spain" appears. More poems, characterized by Alice's ability to give feeling to all situations, continue from page 39 to page 48, where the letter "No Woman Is An Islandess," casually appears, followed by "My Bodyguard," the first of her dialogues based on her everyday life. From pages 62 through 76, short plays appear, which skip lightly from subject to subject, followed by the long title piece, "Waltzing Matilda," diary entries containing free associated observations, dialogues and letters. Her "Interview With George Schneeman" takes up almost the rest of the book, concluding with, the beautiful poem on poets and death, "World's Bliss."

On Nov. 4th, Joe Ceravolo came over with his manuscript, *Millenium Dust*; and, the next day, I picked the paper and cover stock for *Night*

Flight. A couple of days later, we had lunch with the Eshlemans; and, on the 12th, I gave a dinner party for the Berrigans, the Ferraris and Susan Hall. The next day I had lunch with Galen Williams of Poets and Writers; and, the day after that, we had dinner at the Schwartzes'. On the 15th, we had brunch at the Goldbergs'; and, on the 19th, we gave a party at the office to show our new paintings, most of which were hung there. On the 1st of December, we went to Lotte Lenye's funeral. She had died of cancer after a prolonged illness and was buried next to Kurt Weill. It was a real bring down for us. The next day I finally OK'd all the pictorial pages of *Night Flight*; they had needed much correction. On the 11th, I gave a dinner party for Anne and her husband, Reed Bye, Richard Kalina and his wife, Valerie Jaudon, also a painter, and Gerard and his date. It was a great evening. On the 17th, I OK'd the salt print and cover layout for *Night Flight*; and, on the 21st, we went to Larry Rivers' Christmas party.

CHAPTER VII

1982-1988

From the 11th of January, 1982 to the 26th, we were in Europe. On Feb. 1st, Joe Ceravolo came to go over his proofs; and, the next day, I went to a benefit for the Poetry Project at the Marlborough gallery. A few days later, I went to see our newly acquired Susan Hall, "Celebration Night," installed in Louis' apartment; and, on the 9th, my 55th birthday, the publication party for *Night Flight* took place at the Gotham. This book consists of essays on the poetry of Ted Berrigan, John Wieners, Helen Adam and Jack Kerouac, notes on the Jack Kerouac School of Disembodied Poetics and the records of Giorno Poetry Systems, the long essay on David Antin, originally published as a Swollen Magpie Press pamphlet, an essay on Joe Brainard, both his writing and his art, and the essay "Twelve Paintings In My Collection." The twelve paintings are by Ad Reinhardt, Ellsworth Kelly, Andy Warhol, Frank Stella, Tom Wesselmann, Al Held, Red Grooms, Kenneth Noland, Alex Katz, Jack Youngerman, Jennifer Bartlett and Susan Hall. Susan's painting is on the front cover and Jennifer's is on the back. On the 12th, we took Allen and Peter out to dinner at La Cote Basque; and, on the 18th, we went to the MOMA's 50th birthday party, where Dick Oldenburg, the director of the museum, complimented me on the poetry readings. The next day, Joe Ceravolo came over with his corrected proofs and the covers for *Millenium Dust*, the front cover a drawing by his wife, Mona DaVinci, and the back a photograph of Joe by Vico Giacolone. On the 24th, I gave sorceress Helen Adam a slide show of sorceress Austé's drawings at the Hamilton gallery, in preparation for having them do a collaboration; and, a few days later, we took Rochelle and George to lunch, after which I interviewed George about the late Paul Blackburn.

On March 1st, I received an ecstatic letter from Helen about Austé; and, the next day, we went to dinner at the art dealer Barbara Gladstone's. A couple of days later, I had lunch with John Giorno at La Cote Basque and, the day after that, gave a dinner party for the Schwartzes, Charles Henri Ford and his friend Indra, John Giorno and Carol Bergé. From the 7th to the 18th, we were in California; and, when we returned, I read a great review of *Night Flight* by Jim Brodey in the *Poetry Project Newsletter*. I began to receive a lot of fan mail for *Night Flight*. On the 25th, I began taking notes on Paul Blackburn; and, a couple of days later, we had lunch with Ted and Alice. At the end of the month, we took Barbara Gladstone out to dinner. On the 2nd of April, I went to Anne's 37th birthday party. Frances was there looking very ill. On the 9th, I had lunch at Susan's, and, the next day, went to the New York Book Fair, where Kulchur shared a table with Swollen Magpie. On the 14th, I signed a codicil to my will leaving all my literary materials to Columbia, and, on the 23rd, had lunch at Gerard's. The next day, we had lunch with Rochelle and George, and I interviewed George on Blackburn again. A couple of days later, I started writing on Blackburn. At the end of the month, I went to a luncheon for the Center for Visual History, an organization formed for putting poetry on television, hosted by James Laughlin at the Century Club. On May 3rd, the publication party for *Millenium Dust* took place at the Gotham.

Unlike Joe's former work, *Millenium Dust* is a book of night and death, perhaps the end of the universe. He believes there is something beyond us, though it is totally unknowable and cares nothing for its creation; and the second deity is a personal God. He says that if we could get along without the personal God, we would be better off. Love is purely human; though to be human is divine. Love helps resolve his desolation; though it is both desolate and is a thing of beauty and terror. The ocean, the desert and the mountains are key images. The first section of the book is desolation, the second the handling of love and the third the wish for freedom. In the first section, "Winds of the Comet," he speaks of loneliness, darkness and imprisonment. He reaches out for contact and doesn't find it. The cosmos is cold and far away. He tries to think of nature, but "all that's left is rain." He gives himself up to salt; his soul is outside him. In the second section, "Apollo in the Night," he speaks of being beaten up by love. He speaks of crawling to the loved one, of being "wiped out." He asks "what eros of a living star" holds the heavens together, but is himself plagued and lonely. He is alone while he holds his beloved. He pays homage to the song of the wolf. Suffering, pain, poverty, disease, inhumanity, and inequality are all transcendable by a forceful and mysterious life force. In the last section, "Millenium Dust," the rain is over which has reached flood proportions. He senses his own and nature's togetherness. He identifies with the coyote's song. On Good Friday, he goes to a black bar and finds connection there. He hymns the ocean. Pain penetrates but is resolved by love. Despite so much bad luck, the spirit gives us life.

On May 6th, Michael McClure arrived, handsome and charming as ever, to stay at our home during his reading at the MOMA. Because of the renovation at the museum, the readings were to be held at an alternative space that year, and they were all to be videotaped. Michael told us his daughter was pregnant and Philip Whalen was to officiate at her wedding. On the 8th, we took him out to dinner; and, after that, he was out both day and evening most of the time. On the 10th, the first poetry reading of the season took place with Michael and Diane Diprima. It was magnificent. Diane read from the "Loba," and Michael read some great poems, opening first with the Prelude to the Canterbury Tales in middle English. My interview was also good and was given much space on the tape. On the 14th, at Morty's 40th reunion at the University of Pennsylvania, I was standing on a porch that collapsed and took a 22 foot drop. I sustained a nasty compound fracture of my left tibia. I was in a vise for eight weeks and then in a cast. From the 14th to the 29th, I was in the hospital and received many visitors and flowers. Morty took over the introductions at the second and third readings. Paul Violi conducted the interview with Robert Duncan and Ed Dorn, and Bernadette Mayer did the same for Anne Waldman and Taylor Mead.

On June 5th, Ted Berrigan and Steve Carey visited me and, later that day, Eugene and Barbara Schwartz. A couple of days later, Susan Hall visited me, and, the next day, Eduardo Costa, the Argentinian poet who had made the gold earrings I am wearing on the cover of *Kulchur Queen*. On the 9th, Anne visited me, and Morty took her to the dinner dance at the MOMA in my place. On the 14th, Gerritt visited me; and, a few days later, Susan Howe came over to discuss her book,

The Defenestration of Prague. Between June 22nd and July 22nd, I received visits from Gerard, John Giorno, Eduardo, Susan and Pat Whitman. Michael telephoned me on July 21st. On the 11th of August, feeling overheated, but unable to shower because of my cast, my nurse gave me an alcohol rubdown. Some of the alcohol got into my nightgown; and, when I lit a match to smoke a cigarette, it ignited. I was burned on 30% of my body. Morty rolled me in a blanket to put out the flames and saved my life. I was in the burn center at New York Hospital until Sept. 3rd. While in intensive care, when I had only a 50% chance of surviving, I had a room and a nurse to myself, a male nurse who was very compassionate. Afterwards, still not allowed to leave the burn center, I was put in a four person dormitory with three black men. Ther was no hint of sexual awareness; we all just lay there like meat. Neither was there any hint of racist or sexist prejudice; burns are a great leveler. When I got home, finally, I received visits from Paul Violi, Barbara Gladstone, Ted Berrigan, Alice Notley, Carol Goldberg and Susan Hall.

On Oct. 10th, the Violis came for lunch, and Paul and I made plans for the next season's poetry readings. A couple of days later, I gave a cocktail party for Poets & Writers before their annual big benefit. The guest list was much smaller than that for one of my own big parties, and the crowd was much tamer. On the 22nd, I had lunch with Susan Hall; and, from Oct. 22nd to Nov. 1st, we were in California, my first trip on a plane since I had broken my leg. When we returned, Poets & Writers gave us a dinner on a yacht to reciprocate for the cocktail party; and, the next day, Susan Howe came over with her manuscript. On the 12th, we had dinner at the Schwartzes', where Rene carried on outrageously. He said he couldn't tell whether his boy friend was circumcised or not because his cock was so hard. On the 13th, we had lunch with George Economou; and, on the 26th, we had dinner with the Schwartzes and the Kardons. The next day, I bought another Austé and another Randy Stevens. At the end of the month the Merrills came for lunch in the country. On Dec. 2nd, I went to Susan Hall's studio to study her paintings in order to write an essay on them. That evening, we went to a party for the sculptor, Sylvia Stone. On the 11th, the Rothenbergs and Bernard Heidsieck came over to discuss Polyphonix with me. This was an organization, headed by Jean-Jacques Lebel, which put on international poetry readings in Paris. Jean-Jacques, after inquiring about doing Polyphonix in New York, was recommended to me by both Michael McClure and John Giorno. On the 16th, I went to Susan Hall's studio to take more notes on her paintings; and, a couple of days later, we went to her Christmas party. Toward the end of the month, I visited Ted and Alice and had dinner at Holly's. On December 30, I visited John Giorno at 222 Bowery, and had a glass of champagne.

From the 8th to the 22nd of January, 1983, we were in Europe. When we returned, I worked on Susan Howe's proofs. On Feb. 3rd, I took further notes on Susan Hall's paintings; and, the next day, we went to a party at the Walsh's after Neil Welliver's opening at Marlborough. The day after that, Matthew Clarke showed me the tapes from the previous season's poetry readings. Although all of my videotapes appeared on public access televison, Channel D, none of them were sold to other television stations. I therefore discontinued videotaping the readings. On the 18th, I bought a photograph by Ellen Brooks; and, on the 23d, I took more notes on Susan Hall's paintings at her gallery. Pattern and decoration having become unfashionable in the early 80's, I found it difficult to adjust to the expressionism of the period and my collector's instinct floundered for a while.

On March 2nd, I began my essay on Susan Hall; and, a couple of days later, we had lunch with Jean-Jacques, who had come to New York to discuss Polyphonix with me. On the 10th, I had lunch with Richard Bosman and his dealer, Brooke Alexander. A few days after that, I interviewed Barry Yourgrau for my introduction to him at the MOMA, and watched the McClure-DiPrima videotape on Channel D. The day after, I had lunch with John Giorno at Le Colonne D'Or; and, on the 20th, I watched the other two readings on Channel D. A few days later I interviewed both John Yau and Tim Dlugos, and, in the evening, had dinner with Susan Hall and her boyfriend, Paul. On the 24th, I had lunch with Helen Adam. A few days later I interviewed Paul Violi, and on the 31st, had dinner with the Schwartzes.

On April 2nd, we had dinner with Congressman Ben Gilman, and asked him for aid in getting grant money for Polyphonix; and, the next day, had dinner with Meredith Monk. On the 6th, the first poetry reading of the season took place at the MOMA. I introduced Eileen Myles and

Barry Yourgrau; they were both exceptionally good. On the 7th, I had lunch with Gerard, on the 9th, with Ted and Alice and, on the 12th, with Barbara Gladstone and Miriam Schapiro, after which I visited Miriam's studio. That evening, I went to a meeting of Poets & Writers. On the 13th, the second poetry reading of the season took place. I introduced Tim Dlugos and John Yau. Though they both are very good poets, they both were very poor readers. On the 15th, we had dinner at the Economous', and, on the 19th, at Barbara Gladstone's. On the 20th, the third poetry reading of the season took place, followed by a reception. I introduced Paul Violi and Philip Whalen. Paul was good, and Whalen was superb. I announced the next year's International Festival at the reading. Allen Ginsberg told me I should do other internationals, including Russia and China. At the end of the month we had lunch with Anne and Reed; and, on May 2nd, the publication party for Susan Howe's *Defenestration of Prague* took place.

Defenestration of Prague is a very literary book. The beautiful wrap-around cover is by Inigo Jones, "Cloud Containing Divine Poesy," from "Temple of Love: The Queen's Shrovetide Masque, Feb. 10, 1635." "Tuning the Sky" contains a group of language poems. "Speeches at the Barriers" is a series of poems unusually assonant and musical, as contemporary American poetry goes, with much allusion to myth. One is reminded of Paul Balckburn, though I doubt that he was an influence. "Bride's Day" is an even more intensely musical poem, full of alliteration and assonance and saturated with myth. There follows a long section pertaining to Swift's Stella, both in prose and verse, followed by a section on Lear and Cordelia in verse. Both sections are rooted in myth and structured in sound. "God's Spies" is a play with the characters Stella, Cordelia and and the ghost of Swift. Language poems dominate the last section of this intense and beautiful book. Though the literary influences in this book are mostly English and Irish, the author is nevertheless firmly rooted in American language and literature and has written an important book on Emily Dickinson.

On the 6th of May, I had the first of my five plastic surgery operations and was in the hospital most of the month. On the 23rd, Andrei Codrescu came over for a fascinating interview and accepted my essay on Susan Hall for *Exquisite Corpse*. On the last day of the month, Michael McClure arrived for a three day visit and brought me an inscribed copy of his new book. He had dinner with us and spent the evening with us the first day and, the next day, was out on professional business. He sat and talked with us a while in the evening and then went out again. Tony Towle brought his manuscript over on June 2nd, which was our 34th anniversary. We had food in from La Caravelle, while Michael went out. I had given him my key. The next day he left early in the morning. A week later, Susan Hall came for lunch; and, a few days later, I began taking notes on Andrei's poems.

From the 19th of June to the 5th of July, we were in London and La Reserve. On July 6th we had lunch in Paris at Francoise and Bernard Heidsieck's. We had dinner that evening with John Giorno at Le Tour D'Argent, who was also present at lunch, where we discussed Polyphonix. On the 8th we had lunch with Jean-Jacques and, of course, had further discussion of Polyphonix. The next day we flew home and received the awful news that Ted Berrigan had died. This was a shock, as Ted's friendship and poetry had meant a great deal to me. He had seemed like a man who would never die. During the rest of the month, I worked on my essay on Andrei; and, on Aug. 5th, Tony came over with his proofs for *New and Selected Poems*. That weekend, Susan Hall and Paul Pecault came to the country for the weekend; and, a few days later, I visited Richard Bosman's studio with Brooke Alexander. On the 19th, I studied Bosman's paintings in Brooke's gallery; and, at the end of the month, the Violi's came to lunch.

On Sept. 1st, 1983, we had dinner with the Schwartzes. On the 10th, we went to a party at Barbara Gladstone's new temporary loft. It was in a dreadful neighborhood, but much of the art world was there. On the 15th, I started writing on Bosman, and, the next day, had lunch with Allen Ginsberg and Bob Rosenthal to discuss future international poetry readings in collaboration with the Committee for International Poetry. A few days later, we went to the opening of Holly's new uptown gallery, which we thought was a design disaster; and, on the 25th, we went to Poets & Writers' garden party at Robert Rushmore's "Ballroom" in Tuxedo Park. This was an elegant affair, with music and hors d'oeuvres; but the drinks were for sale. After a while, the local cops, probably disliking the arty crowd, appeared with drawn guns, on the grounds that liquor was being sold without a license. All the guests were atwitter. Rushmore told the cops that drinks would then be free, and everyone settled down again. On Oct. 4th, I visited Alice, deeply in mourning, and, on the 11th, had lunch with Helen and Austé. On the 19th, the art department of the University of Pennsylvania gave an exhibition of Kulchur books, followed by a dinner in my honor. On the 26th, I had lunch with Galen and Lisa; and, on the 31st, the publication party for Tony's *New and Selected Poems* took place at the Gotham. It is to be noted that I have written less than formerly about this time period, as I was not well and not doing as much.

Tony Towle is an official member of the second generation New York School, since he was a protegé of Frank O'Hara and a Tibor DeNagy author. His *New and Selected Poems* is a very witty book. The narratives skip in the approved manner. The front cover is a cityscape by Jean Holabird; the back cover is a photograph of Tony by David S. Kelley. In "The Adventure," the lover and his lady are together first among trees, then at sea, then on a pier, then at a river watching a washerwoman, then composing music; finally the meeting breaks up. It is all a metaphor for our discontinuous experience. Similarily, in "Poem," the sky is first cut into sections, then covered with clouds, machines enter the picture and the sky blends together, a river flows down from a mountain, a winding road appears, fish, people in shops and streets appear, clouds and sky reappear. It is all summed up in this comment on our lives: "The next four years show great achievement. The remaining years are disappointing." Thus wit and wisdom are joined.

On Nov. 5th, Yuki Hartman came over to discuss his book. A few days later, I visited John Giorno at 222 Bowery, had a glass of champagne, and left my earrings there. When a black messenger was dispatched from the office the next day to pick them up, he was afraid of the neighborhood. A few years later the building, like most of New York, went expensively cooperative; and John Giorno bought both his and William Burroughs' loft called the Bunker. On the 15th, I had Helen and Austé for lunch, and, in the evening, went to Ted's memorial at the church. I read two of his sonnets. At the end of the month, I bought another Schapiro and payed a visit to Anne Waldman. On the 5th of December, I had the last of my plastic surgery operations, but it was to be a few more years before I recovered my energy. On the 10th, my essay on Susan Hall came out in *Exquisite Corpse*; and, a few days later, Allen brought some Indian dignitaries over to discuss our doing a series of readings at the MOMA for the forthcoming Festival of India. Soon after that, I wrote my little essay for *Best Minds*, a book which was to be published in honor of Allen's 60th birthday.

From Jan. 7, 1984 to the 25th, we were in Europe. On the 15th, we had lunch with the Heidsiecks and Jean-Jacques in Paris; and, on the 22nd, we also had dinner with them. The next day, I went to the Minister of Literary Affairs with Jean-Jacques to try to get grant money for Polyphonix; and, the day after that, we had lunch at his father's apartment, a great art historian with a fabulous collection ranging from the 12th century to Duchamp. After our return home, I had lunch with Anne and Susan to discuss their doing a collaboration, like the one in the works by Helen and Austé. A week later, we had dinner with the Solomons; and, the next day, the artist Sue Green, Yuki's wife, came over with his proofs for the book, *Ping*. A couple of days later, I had a delightful day doing the rounds of Soho with Barbara Gladstone and Rene.

On March 1st, I had Helen and Austé for lunch to discuss their book. Austé's drawings were fabulous, and Helen had many new poems in her incomparably eccentric style. A couple of days later, we bought another Bosman. From the 4th to the 11th, we were in California; and, the very next day, we flew to Washington. There, with Ben Gilman's aid, we conferred with Charles Wick of the USIA and Frank Hodsoll of the NEA about grant money for Polyphonix. The 21st, was a big day. I had lunch with Pat, went to Holly's for cocktails and then went to the Whitney, where our Brad Davis "Black Orchid" was on display. Afterwards, we had dinner at Tom Armstrong's. At the end of the month, we bought a Cham Hendon; art collecting was picking up again. On the 5th of April, I had lunch with Alice, and, the next day, had a conference with Helen and Austé. A couple of days later, I met with Allen and Anne and various Indian dignitaries at the Carlyle Hotel. Art collecting continued, and, in the middle of the month, we bought two Shari Urquarts and a Denis Cardon. On the 21st, I arranged Helen's poems with Austé's drawings; and, on the 23rd, I was photographed by Ned Smythe for a portrait he was to do of me in mosaic. The next day, Austé brought over her gorgeous title page and cover; and, on the 25th, the publication party for Yuki's book, *Ping*, took place at the Gotham.

Ping, is a book of lovely, easily available poems, full of warm feeling and love. The strong, gushing rhythm of these poems reflects Yuki's enthusiasm for life. "Letters," the opening poem, tells of Yuki's love and friendship for those who wrote the letters for him. "Chinatown Sonata," is a comic masterpiece. In "Red Rice," pleasure in a simple meal is a metaphor for love. In "Calligraphy," "bright crimson," "true waterfall," and "swelling leaves," are metaphors for the poet's creation. There is also an admonition against rewriting and a word put in for spontaneity. In the beautiful poem, "Muddy River," the passion of creation, as expressed by the "stars hurled back into space" and "rocks of blinding light," gives way to normal consciousness. Yuki deserves more recognition than he has had.

During the month of May, I began to feel sick with what I thought at first was only bronchitis complicated by my chronic asthma. On June 6th, I collapsed with congestive heart failure, brought on, I think, by the weakness caused by my burns and my many operations. I was in the hospital for most of the month. Recovering in July, I had lunch with Gerard on the 12th, and worked on the Adam/Austé collaboration for most of the month. On the 23rd, I was photographed by Ned Smythe again, since I had gotten thinner in the hospital. At the end of the month, the Merrills came to lunch in the country. On Aug. 3rd, although I should not have done this in my condition, I interviewed Austé in a friend's non-airconditioned loft for three hours. The next week, John Giorno and his friend, Paul Alberts, came to lunch in the country; and, on the 17th, Blake's rehearsal dinner took place. On the 18th, he was married to Elizabeth Reamer, and I was as happy for him as I had been for Louis. I wore a Nina Ricci haute couture original for his wedding as well; but it had to be finished in New York, because my illness postponed our summer visit to Paris. In nine years, the price of such a dress had gone from $800.00 to $5,000.00

On Aug. 24th, we had dinner with Allen. I told him that in 1962, at a reading by George Oppen, he had frowned at me and said, "What are *you* doing here?" He said he didn't remember. On the 26th, we flew to Paris, and, after some time at La Reserve, flew back to Paris on Sept. 13th. There, we had lunch with Jean-Jacques, and discussed Polyphonix again. He came to New York soon after our return; and, on the 19th, I went to an opening at the MOMA with him, followed by a meeting at the office the next day and a meeting with him and Pat the day after. On the 22nd, we brought him to the country for the weekend, followed by a visit to a Larry Rivers opening and a meeting at the French Cultural Embassy. On Oct. 5th, I started writing my essay on Austé. A few days later, we bought Bosman's "Besieged," and, the next day, went to the opening of Meredith Monk's "The Games." I had another lunch date with Jean-Jacques on the 16th, and, on the 18th, had lunch with John Myers, who had at last renewed his friendship with me. On the 20th, the Historical Society of Rockland County toured our country house; and, on the 22nd, the publication party for Helen's and Austé's *Stone Cold Gothic* took place at the Gotham.

I can't express enough enthusiasm for *Stone Cold Gothic*. As in *Turn Again To Me*, Helen uses the ballad form to tell tales of the supernatural, passion, revenge, sorcery, demons, witches, love, sado-masochism and Armageddon. Austé's drawings are perfectly matched to her poems. Austé is a superb draughtsman; and, in her great curving line full of curlicues, and her powerful black and white contrasts, she creates beautiful sorceresses, cats, demons, strange curvilinear flowers, plants, buildings and aerial disturbances. "The Witch's Daughter," tells of the love of a sorceress for a cruel demon. "Grain of Hope Rime, At The End of the World," postulates all hell let loose through the atom's destruction but adds that none of this actually exists. "Song Before Sleep" is an horrific poem about a great house haunted by spiders and a jealous husband smothering his beautiful wife beneath their webs. In "The Copper Key," full of mystery, twin sorceresses destroy a lover. In "The Game of Croquet," beautiful Belinda harries her lover's skull with her mallet, while her proud suitors flatter her. "Ginger Jack's Warning" tells of Silk and Luck, one black and one blond, doing the devil's work by seducing and destroying all the town's men both young and old. In the title poem, the proud prince of the Villa Malcontenta loses his mistress to the great god Anubis. "The Small One" is a fiend who perches on one's thumb to tell "the secrets of deep hell." Tiny though he is, his shadow is huge. In "Low Spoken Warning," sated lovers in the "Mansion of Fulfillment" are disturbed by the purring of the "Hell Cat." Helen's absolute control of her rhymed and metered verse impales the reader on her evocations of lust and terror.

On Oct. 23rd, I had dinner at the loft of Antonio Racelconti, the painter with whom Jean-Jacques was staying. A few days later, I had Anne Waldman and Susan Hall to lunch to discuss their collaboration, and, the next day, Michael arrived to stay with us during the performance of Polyphonix. Thus the International Poetry Festival finally opened on the 29th and continued for five consecutive days. The French poets were Julien Blaine, Jean Francois Bory, Jacqueline Cahn, Michael Deguy, Edouard Glissant, Felix Guattari, Tran Quang Hai, Bernard Heidsieck, Joel Hubaut, Tahar Ben Jelloun, Joelle L'eandre, Jean-Jacques Lebel, Gherasim Luca, Michele Metail, Tibor Papp and Ghedalia Tazartes. The poets from Italy were Guilia Niccolai, Antonio Port and Sarenco. Those from Holland were Bart Chabot, Lydia Schauten and Bert Schreebeck; and, from West Germany, there was Eberhard Blum. On the whole, the European poets seemed retardaire compared to the Americans. The Americans reading were Helen Adam, John Ashbery, Amiri Baraka (LeRoi Jones), John Cage, Andrei Codrescu, Gregory Corso, John Giorno, Richard Howard, Kenneth Koch, Rochelle Kraut, Gerard Malanga, Bernadette Mayer, Michael McClure, Alice Notley, Rochelle Owens, Bob Rosenthal, Jerome Rothenberg, Paul Violi, Anne Waldman and Lewis Warsh. LeRoi, Julian and Helen gave particularly stirring performances. The fifth reading on Nov. 2nd, was followed by a reception at the French Cultural Embassy, where I was awarded the Medalion D'Or pour Des Artes et Des Lettres. The next day, I started editing Anne's and Susan's book; and, on the 13th, we had our last dinner with Jean-Jacques.

Between Jan, 4th 1985 and the 19th, we were in Europe. On the 18th, we had lunch with Francoise and Bernard Heidsieck in Paris. On the 25th, I began reading John Giorno's manuscript, *Grasping At Emptiness*, in preparation for the collaboration planned with him and Richard Bosman. On Feb. 5th, I had lunch with John at 222 Bowery, and had my first view of Burroughs' Bunker, which John was then occupying as well as his own loft. Burroughs had settled in Kansas. In the middle of the month, we had lunch with the Schwartzes in Soho and then went to the East Village galleries with them, where we bought an Art Nouveau mirror and vanity. A couple of days later, I interviewed Joe Ceravolo; and, on the 20th, started working on his poems. At the end of the month, we heard Allen read at the church and got a signed copy of the *Collected Poems* from him. On March 2nd, we bought an Izhar Patkin from Holly, and, in the evening, went to a party for Neil at the Walshes'. On the 6th, we went to the opening of Gerard's photographs of little girls, called "Purity Without Innocence." At the end of the month, I had lunch with Galen and Lisa and tea at Auste's. At Holly's opening, I approved Ned's drawing for my mosaic portrait. From April 1st, to the 8th, we were in California; and, when we returned, I went to the Spring Dance at the Metropolitan Museum with John Giorno. On the 18th, I interviewed Miriam at her gallery; on the 23rd, I had lunch with John Giorno and Richard Bosman at Lutece; and, on the 29th, the publication party for Anne's and Susan's book *Invention* took place at the Gotham. Prior to that Anne had gone to my printer and asked him to stop the book because of what she claimed to be mistakes by me. When, angrily, I told the printer to go ahead with the book, she wrote me some angry letters threatening to disown the book and even hinted at suing me. Fortunately, we both cooled down eventually. It would have been terrible if such a close friendship of such long standing had been broken up because of this misunderstanding.

Susan's drawings for *Invention* show her to be a fine draughtsman, as always; but I miss the imaginative quality present in her former work. Although Anne and she worked together on the book, matching poem to drawing, sometimes in a literal fashion, there is not the striking similarity of imagination seen in the Helen/Austé or Bosman/Giorno collaborations. I went along with Anne's arrangement of the poems and drawings and changed nothing. If there were errors, either it was the printer's fault or Anne was not careful enough with the proofs. Like her former work, Anne's poems are relatively direct and available compared to some other New York School poets. Although her associations do not skip as rapidly as some others do, her poems are not simple. She is a mistress of her craft; and, as always, her rhythms lend themselves to oral recitation. As she has often said of her work, she writes real American, and puts all of herself into her poems; though not as many simple transcriptions of everyday life appear in this book as in *No Hassles*.

On May 4th, we had dinner at the Schwartzes'; and, on the 13th, we went with Barbara Gladstone to an East Village Restaurant, where Jacqueline Schnabel and Rene Ricard were cooking. A couple of days later, we saw a special guest performance of Meredith Monk's "Quarry." A few days after that, I gave a dinner party for the Solomons, the Alexanders and Barbara Gladstone; and, at the end of the month, I put the Giorno/Bosman book together. On the 4th of June, Miriam Schapiro came to lunch and then went with me to Wendy's to analyse the painting I had given her. Following the Party in the Garden on the

143

12th, I had lunch with Miriam and Wendy and then took Miriam to the office to analyse "Building Block Bouquet." From June 23rd to July 15th, we were in Europe. We did not see Jean-Jacques, nor were there any roses waiting for me in our suite in Paris, as there were before Polyphonix. On the 23rd, I had tea at Charles Henri Ford's, who had added a new boy to his menage; and, on the last day of the month I had lunch with Rochelle.

On Aug. 9th, 1985, John Giorno came to lunch and picked up his proofs; and, on the 17th, the Alexanders came to lunch and picked up Bosman's proofs. A few days later, I collated John's proofs with mine. On Sept. 5th, I started taking notes on Miriam's catalogue, and, in the evening, went to a party at Holly's. On the 14th, we bought a Thomas Lanigan Schmidt; and, a couple of days later, Ned Smythe installed his mosaic portrait of me. On the 2nd, we bought an Alexander Kosmopolov; and, on the 23rd, I corrected the revised proofs of the Giorno/Bosman book. On the 1st of October, I had lunch with Susan. We were still good friends but no longer soul sisters. On the 6th, I had lunch with the Violis, on the 10th with Holly, and, on the 19th, with Miriam and her husband, Paul Brach. That day I interviewed her about "Royal Presence," and, on the 23rd, I wrote my essay on her. On the 26th, we bought a Duncan Hannah; and from Oct. 28th to Nov. 1st, we were in California. On Nov. 11th, the publication party for the Giorno/Bosman collaboration, *Grasping At Emptiness*, took place at the Gotham.

The cover of *Grasping At Emptiness* is from a painting in my collection by Richard Bosman, called "Besieged." It shows a man besieged by bats. This sets the tone for both John's poems and Richard's drawings, which are marvelously coordinated. The book forms a unified commentary on both *our* civilization and man's fate. It is composed of five long poems in John's incantatory style, the first three in single column and the last two in double column. They are "It's A Mistake To Think You're Special," "We Got Here Yesterday, We're Here Now, And I Can't Wait To Leave Tomorrow," "I Resigned Myself To Being Here," "Grasping At Emptiness" and "Life Is A Killer." Richard's drawings contain a great many skulls, plus incarcerated figures, struggling, fighting or seeking men, coffins, abused women, snakes, screams, chains, bats, savages, threats of drowning, wild cats, torture, sea monsters, vultures and all the phantasmagoria of nightmare, in heavy black and white contrasts. Richard's nightmares add another dimension to John's despair.

On Dec. 2nd, I went over Rochelle's manuscript, at that time conceived as a collaboration with Miriam's drawings. In the month of January, 1986, I had lunch with Ted Greenwald, who took me to his gallery, and Meredith Monk, who gave me photographs and a score to illustrate the essay I planned to write on her. In February, we went to the opening of the Elaine Sturtevant show at White Columns, curated by Gene Schwartz, followed by a loft party; on the 18th, I had lunch with John Giorno at La Caravelle; and later in the month lunched with Ted Greenwald, Bob Rosenthal and Pat Whitman. In March, I attended Alice's and Michael's reading with Judith Malina, had lunch with Miriam and worked on the manuscript of my next book, *Nine Martinis*. In April, I visited Alice, had lunch with both Miriam and Rochelle and had dinner with Allen. From the 5th of May through the 7th, the Indian/American poetry readings took place at the MOMA. The Indian poets were Gopalakrishna Adiga (Kanrada), Nissim Exekiel (English), Sunil Ganguly (Bengali), Akhtar-Ul-Iman (Urdu), Arun Kolartkar (Marathi and English), Amrita Pritam (Punjabi), Nabeneeta Sen (Bengali) and Keder Noath Singh (Hindi). The American poets were Jayne Cortez, Victor Hernandez Cruz, Maage Dubris, Allen Ginsberg, James Laughlin, David Rattray, Tony Towle, Tom Wiegel and Bill Zavatsky. Cortez and Dubris gave particularly memorable performances.

On May 13th, I had lunch with Alice, and, the next day, started working on the proofs for *Nine Martinis*. At the end of the month we went to the Party in the Garden at the MOMA. On June 11th, I had lunch with Miriam and her dealer, Bernice Steinbaum, and, the next day, sent nine cartons of literary materials to the Columbia Rare Book and Manuscript Library. I had willed them all my literary materials and books upon my death and then decided to send them part of the material before that time. This consisted of letters, manuscripts, proofs, financial records, pictorial matter and miscellaneous material. At the end of the month, I worked on the front cover of *Nine Martinis*, and, on July 3rd, labelled all the color transparencies. Later in the month I had lunch with both Mark Nasdor, of the Committee for International Poetry, and my old friend Gerard.

On Aug. 10th, the Schwartzes came for lunch in the country, bringing their son, Michael, and his fianceé Barbara Salasny. Later in the month, the Violis also came for lunch. On Sept. 6th, Anne Poor brought us a drawing of our country house as a gift for Tripp; and, on the 24th, I went to a private performance and a cognac tasting party for Meredith. On the 30th, I had lunch with John Giorno in the Bunker at 222 Bowery. Early in October, we bought another Duncan Hannah; and, a few days later, I had lunch with Meredith. On the 11th, we had lunch with Micahel Schwartz and Barbara, henceforth known as BZ, and went to galleries with them. We also went to an auction with them, where we placed a bid on a Lichtenstein print and a Kostabi artist's proof. Later in the month, I had lunch with both Susan and Miriam, and, on the 16th, had dinner with Allen. On Nov. 3rd, I had lunch with Pat, who told me of great changes in the Museum. The Associate Council would become the Contemporary Arts Council, and the dues would go up considerably. A few days later, I met with Bob, Simon and Mark at the Hilton to discuss the projected readings of Chinese and American poets at the MOMA. Ben Gilman was supposed to be there but did not show up. On the 8th, I went to see Susan's very disappointing show at Ted Greenwald's gallery, and, the next day, had the Pousette Dart's for lunch. From Dec. 4th to the 11th, we were in St. Martin's, which we hated.

On Jan. 3, 1987, Michael McClure called, "just to hear your voice and gossip." I was deeply moved. On the 17th, we bought one of Sandy Scoglund's first paintings, and, a couple of days later, had dinner with Allen. On the 29th, I went to a cocktail party for Meredith at June Poster's loft, and brought them advance copies of *Nine Martinis*. On Feb. 9th, my 60th birthday, the publication party for *Nine Martinis* took place at the Gotham. There are nine essays in this book, hence the title. There are four essays on poetry: Paul Blackburn, Andrei Codrescu, Joe Ceravolo and Alice Notley, four esseys on painting, each accompanied by eight color plates: Susan Hall, Richard Bosman, Austé and Miriam Schapiro, and a brief essay on the whole art of Meredith Monk, accompanied by photographs of her and her company and the score of "Dolmen Music." Bosman's "Norseman" is on the front cover and Austé's "Hidden Guitar" is on the back cover.

On the day after my publication party, I started working on this memoir; and, on the 19th of February, I had lunch with John Giorno at La Cote Basque. From March 3rd to the 10th, we were in California; and, soon after we came home, I gave a dinner party for the

Schwartzes, the Bosmans, John Giorno and Paul Alberts. In April, I spent most of my time writing. On May 11th, we had dinner with Holly, she having split up with Horace; and, on the 17th, we went to Michael Schwartz's wedding. On June 3rd, we went to a Contemporary Arts Council party at Nell's, and then to the Party in the Garden. From the 8th to the 30th, we were in Europe, spending the first week in Ireland, which we found fascinating. This was the first new country we had gone to in many years. There we saw gold jewelry 5,000 years old, and looking like Mycenaean gold. We visited New Grange, a 5,000 year old tomb, with carving on the walls like the designs in the *Book of Kells*. We also went to Joyce's tower, now a museum, to the cathedral where Swift was buried, and to Lady Gregory's Coole Park, where all the famous Irish writers had inscribed the Autograph Tree.

On July 25th, I finished the first draft of this memoir and set it aside. The next day, Ellsworth Kelly came to lunch with his friend, Jack Shear. Early in August, I had lunch with Allen and Bob, who had just received their first reponse from China. On the 14th, we visited Ultra Violet; and, a couple of days later, John Giorno and Paul Alberts came up to the country for the day. A few days after that, we had dinner at the home of Jerry and Emily Speigel, a couple who recently had become major art collectors; and, on Sept 25th, we went to a party for Bosman at the gallery of his dealer, Brooke Alexander. The next day we bought a Mark Strathey; and, on the 7th of October, we went to the opening of the great Stella show at the MOMA. A couple of days after that, I began working on Rochelle's book, *How Much Paint Does The Painting Need*? Miriam having been too late and having put too many obstacles in the way, I decided to do Rochelle alone. On the 10th, we tried with no success to buy a Peter Halley, there having been none available; and, the next day, we had the Spiegels for lunch. On the 15th, we went to our old friend John Myers' memorial ceremony, he having died of cancer after surviving many years on chemotherapy. On the 23rd, I had lunch with John Giorno in the Bunker and, in the evening, went to a gala for the Rockland Center for the Arts. At the end of the month, we bought a Joanna Pousette-Dart, Richard's daughter, and a second Cham Hendon.

On the 8th of November, we bought a little Beverly Conglan watercolor, and, on the 14th, a Cary Smith. On the 20th, I worked on Rochelle's page proofs and, on the 22nd, went to Meredith's birthday party at BAM. On the 11th of december, I gave a dinner party for Allen, Alice, Joe Brainard, Ultra Violet, Louis and Wendy. The next day, we went to Paul Albert's all Beethoven piano concert at Carnegie Recital Hall, and had supper afterwards at the Russian Tea Room with Paul and John Giorno. On the 10th of January, 1988, we bought two Gilbert Hsiaos, and, on the 19th, had lunch with Holly. A few days later, I gave a dinner party for the Schwartzes, Judith Malina, her director, now her husband, Hanon Reznikov, Blake and Liz. On the 22nd, I had lunch at La Cote Basque with John Giorno and Kynaston McShine, curator of painting and sculpture at the MOMA, and, on the 28th, went to the funeral of Barbara Schwartz's mother. A couple of days later, we paid Barbara a condolence call. On Feb. 1st, I started the second draft of this memoir; and, on the 15th, the publication party for *How Much Paint Does The Painting Need*? took place at the Gotham.

In this book Rochelle remains the primordial singer. The cover, designed by myself, has a bright red ground and bold black type. There is much about painting in this book, probably because it was originally intended as a collaboration with Miriam Schapiro; though, of course, Rochelle knows a great deal about the psychology of painting, as her first husband, Owens, was an abstract expressionist. There are also, as always in Rochelle's work, many allusions to history and pre-history. Out of this, Rochelle both refers to myth and creates myth. Farsi is the language most often referred to; and the Persian, Saud, is the most important character in this matrix of multiple allusions. The book ends with a long poem dedicated to Willem de Kooning.

On the 19th of February, we had lunch with Rochelle and showed her around the Soho galleries. At Koury Wingate we bought the first of our two Serge Kliavings. On the 23rd, I had lunch with Bob, Mark and Simon to further discuss the Chinese poetry readings; and, a few days later, we had lunch with Pat Whitman. On the 16th of March, we went to the Gotham to go over the appraisal of my literary materials with Andreas Brown; and, on the 22nd, we brought the necessary legal papers to Kenneth A. Lohf the director of the Rare Book and Manuscript Library. A few days later, we met with Anita Tiburzi of Atwood International, a public relations firm, in order to publicize the important Chinese-American readings and, by way of background material, the work of the Kulchur Foundation. On the 1st of April, we went to the Living Theatre Seder, and, the next day to the opening of a Warhol exhibit, curated by Gerard, to which we lent our Nixon poster, reading "Vote McGovern," and at which the photographs for *Screen Tests* were displayed. On the 6th, we had dinner at the Schwartzes', and, the next day, had lunch with Ultra Violet. On the 8th, Ealan Wingate came to see our collection and bring our second Serge Kliaving with him; and, on the 10th, we heard Allen read at the church. On the 11th, I audited his class at Brooklyn College, at which Anne Waldman and Karl Rakosi both read and lectured.

Anne started out by praising Don Allen's anthology, which she said was not in the same world as Lowell or Nemeroff, who taught her at Bennington. She then read from some Tibor DeNagy editions and told of her experience at the Berkeley Poetry Conference. She said her influences were Stein, Berrigan and the objectivists, not Pound at first. Allen then asked her what women writers she had dredged up, to which she replied Noreen Niedecker, H.D., Stein and Mina Loy. Karl then said his early influences were Eliot, Pound's critical works, Williams, Cummings, his socialist father, Stevens and Crane. His social work led him to Marxism, which destroyed his poetic impulse for twenty-seven years. Allen then said his family were communists who accused his father of being a bourgeois lyricist. He also said that theoreticians do not know what real poetry is. Karl added that Trotsky had warned his followers to leave the arts alone. Allen then said that the communists believe that you should not inflict your ego on the masses, and that the Buddhists believed the same thing. He added that the language poets suppressed subjectivity and that the greatest Stalinists in this country were the moral majority, because they censored pornography. The neo-conservatives were authoritarian, like the communists, objecting to the expression of the ego and wanting to control reality. Karl then said that the letter of Andrew Crozier, who had studied with Olson at Buffalo, was what sent him back to writing poetry again. He said that Rexroth was the originator of the rumor that he had died behind the Iron Curtain. Anne then asked if he thought writing in isolation was possible, to which he was noncommittal. As to the issue of whether the poet was a private or public person, he said that Oppen did not like reading in public, and that he himself did not like readings at first but now did. Allen added that at Naropa he taught reading into deeper and deeper silence. Anne then said that at Berkeley, the large numbers of poets and their improvisations were very inspiring. She added that both books and readings were important to her, to which Allen agreed. He added that some poems were musical, some like collages and some objectivist. Anne then read a list poem, in her usual theatrical style, and answered a student's question about Frank O'Hara by saying that he was characterized by great surface energy, going on his nerve, a love of art and a love of friends. They then discussed the issues of active vs. passive attitudes and masculine vs. feminine. Anne said that the Reagan regime was masculine, and Allen added that Jeane Kirkpatrick was a man. He concluded by saying that the first half of this century was modern and the second half post modern.

On the 14th of April, we went to see Jerome Rothenberg's poem "Poland 1931," adapted for the stage by Hanon Reznikov, and presented by the newly reopened Living Theatre. A couple of days later, we bought our second Ian Hornak; and, on the 20th, I had lunch with Ken Stuart and Juanita Lieberman of Paragon House Publishing. On the last day of the month we had lunch with Judith and Hanon; and, on May 3rd, Kenward Elmslie and Joe Brainard came to lunch with the manuscript and drawings for their collaboration, *Sung Sex*. Morty had an operation on the 11th; and, from then until the 19th, I spent my days in the hospital. On the 24th, I went to the office to have the letters to poets typed for the fall poetry readings; and, on the 30th, I brought the second draft of this memoir as far as it could go for the time being.

On June 1st, Morty died of a sudden completely unexpected heart attack, and my whole life changed forever. He had had a colon cancer operation on May 11th, and had been told he had had a *complete cure*. On June 1st, the day before our 39th anniversary, he keeled over in his chair and died. The colon operation had been very painful, and he bore his pain stoically. I will always honor him for that. Fortunately, his death was painless. It was too sudden for him to have any awareness of it; it would have been awful for him to have died of a lingering disease. His funeral was on June 3rd at Campbell's, followed by a burial in Haverstraw near his factory. I recited Shakespeare's sonnet XV and Dylan Thomas' "Do Not Go Gentle Into That Good Night" at the service.

From June 3rd through the rest of the month, I received a stream of condolence callers. On the 15th, I attended a gala benefit at The

Kitchen, a video and performance art organization, escorted by John Giorno. The Schwartzes and the Bosmans were present. I was not yet ready to go out in the evening and had a bad time at the party. On the 19th, I fell down in Anne Poor's House and broke my ankle. There followed six days of confinement in the hospital, after which I was confined to my apartment till July 25th. I received many visitors. On August 15th, contrary to his promise, Dr. Lyden refused to remove my cast. On the 17th, I went for a second opinion to Dr. Pruzansky. He agreed to take it off in another week. On the 24th, he replaced the cast with a removable brace. On Sept. 3rd, I flew to London for an eight day trip with Louis, Wendy and Tripp. It did a lot to lift my sprits.

On September 12th, I corrected the final proofs for Kenward and Joe's book, *Sung Sex*, and started working on my introductions for November's poetry readings. On the 14th, I went to the opening of the Thomas Lanigan Schmidt show at Holly's, to which I lent a small icon. The next day, I bought an Allen McCollom sculpture and an April Gornik landscape; and, that evening, Allen Ginsberg took me out to dinner. A week later, I had dinner with Alice Notley and Doug Oliver, and, a few days after that, I went to a Producer's Council meeting of BAM, which I had recently joined. On the 27th, Doug brought me a much sought after copy of *Chapman's Homer*; and Bob Rosenthal and Tony Caine came over to discuss a round table forum at Asia House for both the Chinese and American poets who would be reading at the MOMA.

On October 3rd, I had lunch with Micky Wesson and Jonathan Giles of Meredith Monk's foundation, the board of which I had recently joined. A couple of days later, I went out to dinner with Gerard and then to the opening of the Degas exhibit at the Metropolitan. On the 6th, I became interested in Milan Kunc's painting, "The Sky," at the Robert Miller gallery, and on the 11th, went to a dinner at the Carlyle given by Poets & Writers. The next day I went out to dinner with John Giorno at La Cote Basque and then to the opening of the Kiefer exhibit at the MOMA. On the 14th, I went to Judith Malina's for dinner, and, a few days later, to the Next Wave Gala at BAM with John Giorno. The first section of "The Warrior Ant" was performed there. At all of these occasions John Giorno wore black tie, which he said he really liked. On the last day of the month there was a meeting of Morty's executors; and, the next day, John brought Francoise and Bernard Heidsieck

151

to dinner. On Nov. 2nd, I bought my second Cary Smith at the Koury Wingate gallery and had an interesting conversation with the artist. On the 7th, I had lunch with John and the Heidsiecks, in the Bunker at 222 Bowery. John served boiled lobser on blue 17th Century English export china, with silver and Lalique from his family. I had dinner with Gerard the next evening.

On Nov. 14th, 15th and 16th, a Poetic Exchange, readings by American poets and poets from the People's Republic of China took place at the MOMA, presented by the Contemporary Arts Council and sponsered by the Kulchur Foundation and the Committee for Internal Poetry. It was the climax of my career. On the 14th, the readers were Deborah Boe, Li Gang, Marc Nasdor, Gu Cheng and Alice Notley. On the 15th, they were Simon Pettet, Jiang He, Kathleen Aguero and Antler. On the 16th, Richard Oldenburg, the director of the museum paid a tribute to me and read a letter to me from Mayor Koch. The readers were Michael McClure, Gong Liu, Gary Snyder, Bei Dau and Allen Ginsberg. It was a smash success. Although I will publish a collaboration between Kenward Elmslie and Joe Brainard in February, and Pat Whitman has convinced me to sponsor one more poetry reading next year, I am about to retire from Kulchur after 29 years, almost half my life. I shall keep the Kulchur Foundation alive to sell books and to give grants. The forces are abated that drove me for so long; and I now wish only to devote myself to reading and collecting art. It is time to float downstream.

November 19, 1988
Lita Hornick